Vegetarian Cooking

British Taste

Science of the Soul Research Centre

Published by:
G. P. S. Bhalla
Science of the Soul Research Centre
c/o Radha Soami Satsang Beas
5 Guru Ravi Dass Marg, Pusa Road
New Delhi 110 005, India

For internet orders, please visit:
www.rssb.org

For book orders within India, please write to:
Radha Soami Satsang Beas
BAV Distribution Centre, 5 Guru Ravi Dass Marg
Pusa Road, New Delhi 110 005

First edition 2014

21 20 19 18 17 16 15 14   8 7 6 5 4 3 2 1

ISBN 978-93-80077-40-6

Printed in India by: Lakshmi Offset Printers

CONTENTS

Sides 107

Breads 123

Condiments

Desserts

INTRODUCTION

When pursuing a spiritual life, which has at its core the love of God, wouldn't we want our lifestyle to reflect our ideals? If we accept that all creation is His, then we need to celebrate his creation, not harm it. A vegetarian diet that holds all life to be sacred is a first step on our journey towards God realisation. With a commitment to being vegetarians--eating no animal products, including meat, fish, fowl, eggs and anything that contains their by-products—we are making a clear and significant statement that our priority is to honour God and his creation. We are saying that instead of living in a world of exploitation, we are living in a world of love.

As vegetarians we are practicing a lifestyle of compassion and kindness, not only in our personal life but also in relationship to the life of the planet. A vegetarian diet makes less of a negative impact on the resources and health of the earth and helps support the ethical treatment of animals. Positive moral choices have significance far beyond our own personal horizon.

When life is full of responsibilities and too overwhelming, we need to find those activities that can give us a sense of peace and calm. There is something nurturing and satisfying about preparing a meal for loved ones. Even taking a little time to cook for ourselves can dissolve the stress of the day and give us a sense of well-being that is beyond the goodness of the food itself.

We live in a time in which we are at risk of losing a sense of intimacy and connection. Family meals are a time to relax and enjoy each other's company and to nurture community and love. Cooking is a wonderful chance to cultivate these values and also to be creative and experimental; therefore we have included variations of some recipes to inspire a new culinary journey. We have tried to keep these recipes as simple and tasty as possible.

As culture within Britain has diversified, so too has its food. We have, therefore, included both traditional British recipes as well as recipes that reflect the modern British population. These have been flavoured to embrace what we now consider to be British taste.

Most importantly - enjoy!

DIETARY INFORMATION

This book has been designed to be user friendly and practical. The following symbols are used throughout the book to identify recipes that are suitable for specific diets:

Gf = Gluten free
A diet that excludes the protein gluten, found in grains such as wheat, barley, rye and triticale. The diet is a treatment for coeliac disease.

Lf = Lactose free
A diet that excludes lactose (a milk sugar) found in products such as milk, cream and some cheeses.

V = Vegan
A diet that excludes meat, eggs, dairy products and all other animal derived ingredients.

Recipes in this book can be made gluten free, lactose free and vegan by substituting certain ingredients. Please feel free to adapt the recipes according to your taste.

WEIGHTS & MEASUREMENTS

TEMPERATURES

°C	°F	Gas
120	250	½
135	275	1
150	300	2
165	325	3
180	350	4
190	375	5
200	400	6
220	425	7
230	450	8
245	475	9

WEIGHTS

g	oz	
30	1	
50	1.8	
100	3.5	
225	8	(½ lb)
455	16	(1 lb)
500	17.6	
750	26.5	
910	32	(2 lbs)
1000 (1kg)	35	

LIQUIDS

ml	fl oz	
10	0.4	
20	0.7	
30	1	
50	1.8	
100	3.5	
125	4.4	(½ cup)
250	8.8	(1 cup)
285	10	(½ pint)
500	17.6	(2 cups)
570	20	(1 pint)
750	26.4	(3 cups)
1000 (1 litre)	35.2	(4 cups)

Please note, the above charts are based on UK measurements. Sizes of cups and weights of ingredients may vary considerably. Numbers have been rounded.

Breakfast

Blueberry Breakfast Scones

Serves 8

170g (6oz)	self-raising flour
60g (2oz)	oatbran
1 tsp	baking powder
30g (1oz)	caster sugar
105ml (3½ floz)	milk
60g (2oz)	butter
60g (2oz)	blueberries

Preheat oven to 220°C/425°F/Gas 7

Method

1. Sift dry ingredients into a bowl.

2. Add milk, butter and blueberries and combine to form soft dough.

3. Shape the dough into a ball and lightly knead.

4. Roll the dough out on a floured surface to 1cm (½ inch) thick and cut out 5cm (2 inch) rounds using a cookie cutter or a small glass.

5. Place the scones on a greased baking tray and bake for 12–15 minutes or until golden brown on top.

➤ Serve with butter, clotted cream and jam.

Lemon Scones
At step 2, replace blueberries with finely grated zest of 1 lemon.

Crystallised Ginger Scones
At step 2, replace blueberries with 60g (2oz) of finely diced crystallised ginger.

Breakfast Potato Scone

Serves 4

220g (8 oz)	potatoes
15g (½ oz)	butter
60g (2 oz)	plain flour
½ tsp	baking powder
½ tsp	salt
1 tbs	oil

Method

1. Peel, wash and chop potatoes into 2cm (1 inch) chunks and cook in boiling water for 7 minutes or until cooked.

2. Drain potatoes in a colander and cool under cold running water.

3. Melt butter in a saucepan then add potatoes and lightly mash.

4. Sift flour, baking powder and salt into the mashed potatoes.

5. Combine mixture, using your hands to form a dough.

6. Roll the dough out on a floured surface to ½cm (¼ inch) thickness.

7. Cut out 2–3 circles using a small plate as a guide, then cut each circle into quarters and prick with a fork.

8. Heat oil in a large frying pan over a medium heat. Place quarters into the frying pan and cook until golden on both sides.

➤ *Serve hot with butter.*

Cheese & Chive Breakfast Potato Scone

60g (2 oz)	cheddar cheese
2 tbs	fresh chives

At step 3, add grated cheese and chopped chives.

Banana & Blueberry Porridge

Serves 2–3

60g (2 oz)	butter
80g (3 oz)	oats
500ml (17½ fl oz)	milk
1	banana
handful	blueberries
½ tsp	ground cinnamon
2 tbs	honey

Method

1. Melt butter in a small saucepan over a low heat. Add oats to the saucepan and cook for 30 seconds, or until slightly toasted, on a medium heat.

2. Add milk to the oats and bring to a boil while stirring occasionally.

3. Reduce heat to low to medium and stir in sliced banana, blueberries and cinnamon.

4. Continue to stir and cook until desired consistency is reached.

➤ *Serve with a drizzle of honey or maple syrup.*

Poached Pear & Orange Porridge

1 tsp	vanilla extract
pinch	ground nutmeg
2	pears
1	orange

1. Place vanilla extract and nutmeg in a saucepan with 250 ml (9 fl oz) of boiling water.

2. Peel, core and cut pears into 2cm (1 inch) chunks and add to the saucepan. Simmer for 5 minutes until soft and tender.

3. Bring to boil, then drain the pears and add to porridge, replacing blueberries and bananas. Add grated zest of an orange.

French Toast

120ml (4½ fl oz)	soya milk
350g (12 oz)	silken tofu
2 tbs	olive oil
2 tbs	maple syrup
1 tsp	ground cinnamon
½	orange
3 slices	bread
	oil for frying

Method

1. Put grated zest of ½ orange, milk, tofu, olive oil, maple syrup and ground cinnamon into a blender and liquidise into a smooth batter.

2. Thoroughly coat each bread slice with batter.

3. Melt butter or heat oil in a frying pan.

4. Fry battered bread slices for a few minutes over a low to medium heat until golden brown on both sides.

➤ *Serve with maple syrup.*

Savoury French Toast
At step 1, replace ground cinnamon, orange zest and maple syrup with 1 tsp of English mustard and salt and pepper to taste.

Pancakes

170g (6 oz)	plain flour
2 tbs	gram flour
1 tsp	baking powder
¼ tsp	salt
175ml (6 fl oz)	milk
175ml (6 fl oz)	water
1 tbs	sunflower oil
	additional oil for frying

Method

1. Sift flour, gram flour, baking powder and salt together in a bowl.

2. Add milk, water and sunflower oil to the bowl and whisk to form a smooth, runny batter. Ensure there are no lumps in the mixture.

3. Let batter sit for at least 5 minutes. Whisk again and add more milk if consistency is too thick.

4. Heat a small amount of oil in a frying pan, until very hot.

5. Pour enough pancake mixture to thinly cover the bottom of the pan. Fry both sides of the pancake over a medium heat for 1 minute or until golden and dry.

➤ *Serve the pancakes drizzled with maple syrup or lemon juice and sugar.*

Filled Sweet Pancakes
Before serving, place fresh berries, sliced banana and ice cream in the centre of the pancake. Roll the pancake, drizzle with syrup of choice and dust with icing sugar.

Filled Savoury Pancakes

2 cloves	garlic
140g (5 oz)	mushrooms
110g (4 oz)	spinach

1. Finely chop garlic and slice mushrooms.

2. Heat a small amount of oil in a frying pan and add garlic and mushrooms. Once almost all the mushroom liquid has evaporated, add spinach and cook until wilted. Place filling in centre of pancake and fold.

French Toast
At step 5, soak slices of bread in pancake batter and fry over a medium-low heat in a non-stick frying pan for a few minutes on each side until golden brown.

Veggie Lincolnshires

½ tbs	gram flour
½ tbs	water
100g (4 oz)	chestnuts
60g (2 oz)	firm tofu
¼	onion
30g (1 oz)	cheddar cheese
small handful	fresh rosemary or sage
¼ tbs	soy sauce
1 tsp	lemon juice
¼ tsp	chilli powder
60g (2 oz)	breadcrumbs
	olive oil for frying

Method

1. Mix gram flour and water together in a small bowl to make a paste and set aside.

2. If using uncooked chestnuts, wash and place in a pot of boiling water and cook for 15–20 minutes. Drain and rinse under cold water. Once cool, peel the outer brown skin and remove the soft nut.

3. Put the chestnuts into a food processor and pulse to a fine crumb.

4. Crumble tofu into a large bowl. Grate onion and cheddar cheese into the tofu.

5. Finely chop rosemary or sage leaves, and add to mixture with soy sauce, lemon juice and chilli powder.

6. Add gram flour paste and breadcrumbs and mix well using a wooden spoon or hands until the mixture is firm.

7. Evenly divide the mixture to 4 sections and roll each into a log.

8. Heat oil in a frying pan. Fry logs in oil over a medium heat, while turning occasionally for 6–7 minutes or until brown.

➤ *Veggie Lincolnshires can be stored in freezer (they are best cooked from frozen), separating the logs with greaseproof paper or baking parchment.*

Scrambled Tofu

110g (4oz)	onion
60g (2oz)	red bell pepper
110g (4oz)	courgette
60ml (2 floz)	olive oil
110g (4oz)	mushrooms
1 tbs	soy sauce
1 tsp	vegetable stock powder
450g (1lb)	firm tofu
½ tsp	turmeric powder
2 tsp	lemon juice
	salt and pepper to taste

Method

1. Dice onions and bell peppers, slice courgettes into rounds and set aside.

2. Heat oil in frying pan, add onions and cook over medium heat for 5-10 minutes or until soft and golden.

3. Slice mushrooms, add to fried onions and cook for 3–4 minutes, then add soy sauce, salt and pepper to taste.

4. Add courgettes, bell peppers, vegetable stock and mix well.

5. Wash and gently squeeze tofu to remove excess water. Crumble tofu and add turmeric powder into the vegetable mixture, and mix well. Add lemon juice and sauté for a few minutes.

6. Cover the frying pan, allow to steam, stirring regularly until peppers and courgettes are tender on a reduced heat.

➤ *Serve with toast.*

Scrambled Tofu with Cheese

½ tsp	English mustard
60 (2oz)	cheddar cheese

At step 6, add English mustard to fried onions and stir well. Grate cheese into tofu after lemon juice and cook until melted.

Breakfast Potatoes

340g (12 oz)	potatoes
2 tbs	olive oil
2 cloves	garlic
1	onion
1 tbs	dried thyme
	salt and pepper to taste

Method

1. Peel and chop potatoes into half-moon shaped slices. Put in a saucepan of boiling water for 5–7 minutes, until fully cooked and tender. Drain and set aside.

2. Finely chop garlic and slice onion. Heat oil in a frying pan, add garlic and onions and fry for a few minutes over medium heat.

3. Add potatoes to the onions and garlic, mix well over a high heat.

4. Add dried thyme, salt and pepper to taste. Fry potatoes, turning them occasionally until crisp golden brown.

➤ *Serve with toast. Also great with scrambled tofu.*

Full English Breakfast

Serves 4

Fried Mushrooms
Grilled Tomatoes
Veggie Lincolnshires
Breakfast Potatoes
Scramble Tofu

Fried Mushrooms

2 cloves	garlic
310g (11 oz)	mushrooms
2 tbs	olive oil
1 tsp	dried thyme or oregano

1. Finely chop garlic and slice mushrooms.

2. Heat olive oil in a frying pan, add garlic and mushrooms, cook for a few minutes over high heat.

3. Add dried herb, cook for another 2 minutes or until the mushrooms are cooked and have reduced in size. Be careful not to overcook the mushrooms as they become sloppy: they should be slightly firm but tender.

Grilled Tomatoes

2	tomatoes
	olive oil for frying
	salt and pepper to taste

1. Cut tomatoes in half, place on a baking tray with the cut side up. Drizzle with olive oil, salt and pepper to taste.

2. Grill the tomatoes until they start to blister around the edges and brown slightly on top under high heat.

Veggie Lincolnshires

½ tbs	gram flour
½ tbs	water

100g (4 oz)	chestnuts
60g (2 oz)	firm tofu
¼	onion
30g (1 oz)	cheddar cheese
small handful	fresh rosemary or sage
¼ tbs	soy sauce
1 tsp	lemon juice
¼ tsp	chilli powder
60g (2 oz)	breadcrumbs
	olive oil for frying

1. Mix gram flour and water together in a small bowl to make a paste and set aside.

2. Wash the uncooked chestnuts, and place in a pot of boiling water and boil for 15–20 minutes. Drain and rinse under cold water. Once cool, peel the outer brown skin and remove the soft nut. Place the chestnut in a food processor and pulse to a fine crumb.

3. Crumble tofu using your hands into a large bowl. Grate onion and cheddar cheese into the tofu.

4. Finely chop rosemary or sage leaves, add to mixture with soy sauce, lemon juice and chilli powder. Add gram flour paste and breadcrumbs and mix well using a wooden spoon or hands until the mixture is firm.

5. Evenly divide the mixture to 4 sections and roll each into a log.

6. Heat a little olive oil in a frying pan, fry logs over a medium heat while turning occasionally for 6-7minutes or until brown.

Breakfast Potatoes

340g (12 oz)	potatoes
2 tbs	olive oil
2 cloves	garlic
1	onion
1 tbs	dried thyme
	salt and pepper to taste

1. Peel and chop potatoes into half-moon shaped slices. Put into a saucepan of boiling water for 5–7 minutes or until fully cooked and tender. Drain and set aside.

2. Finely chop garlic and slice onion.

3. Heat oil in a frying pan, add garlic and onions and fry for a few minutes over a medium heat.

4. Add potatoes to the onions and garlic, mix well over a high heat.

5. Add dried herbs, salt and pepper to taste. Fry potatoes, turning them occasionally until crisp and golden brown.

Scrambled Tofu

110g (4oz)	onion
60g (2oz)	red bell pepper
110g (4oz)	courgette
60ml (2 floz)	olive oil
110g (4oz)	mushrooms
1 tbs	soy sauce
1 tsp	vegetable stock powder
450g (1 lb)	firm tofu
½ tsp	turmeric powder
2 tsp	lemon juice
	salt and pepper to taste

1. Dice onions and bell peppers. Slice courgettes into rounds.

2. Heat olive oil in frying pan, add onions and cook over medium heat for 5-10 minutes or until soft and golden.

3. Slice mushrooms and add to fried onions, cook for 3–4 minutes; add soy sauce, salt and pepper to taste.

4. Add courgettes, bell peppers, vegetable stock and mix well.

5. Wash and gently squeeze tofu to remove excess water. Crumble tofu into vegetables mixture, add turmeric powder and mix well. Add lemon juice and fry for a few minutes.

6. Cover the frying pan, reduce heat and allow to steam, stirring regularly until peppers and courgettes are tender.

➤ *Serve hot with toast and baked beans.*

BTLT (Baked Tofu, Lettuce & Tomato Sandwich)

Makes 2

8–10 slices	baked tofu
4 slices	bread
2 tbs	vegan mayonnaise
4 leaves	lettuce
1	tomato

Baked Tofu

400g (14 oz)	firm tofu
½	lemon
125ml (4½ fl oz)	light soy sauce
3 tbs	sesame oil
110g (4 oz)	fine cornmeal or polenta
1 tbs	dried herbs
	olive oil for drizzling

Preheat oven to 200°C/400°F/Gas 6

1. Place an empty baking tray in the oven to heat.

2. Wash the tofu and gently squeeze to remove excess water.

3. Slice the tofu into 8–10 slices, according to size of bread. Set aside on a paper towel to absorb excess moisture.

4. Mix lemon juice, soy sauce and sesame oil into a small bowl.

5. Place tofu in mixture and set aside to marinate for one hour in fridge.

6. Mix cornmeal or polenta and herbs in a small bowl.

7. Carefully remove the hot baking tray from the oven and evenly cover bottom of tray with oil.

8. Coat marinated tofu with flour and herb mixture and place on hot oiled baking tray.

9. Bake tofu for 15–20 minutes or until golden and slightly crisp, turning once after 10 minutes.

10. Place tofu on bread with other ingredients.

Aloo Paratha

Dough

200g (7 oz)	wholemeal flour
100–125ml (3½ - 4½ fl oz)	water
½ tsp	salt
2–3 tsp	oil

1. Combine wholemeal flour, salt and oil in a medium sized mixing bowl. Add water. Turn the dough out onto a lightly floured surface and knead for 5 minutes or until soft and elastic.

2. Break the dough into 8 equal pieces, and roll each into a ball.

3. Place in a small, oiled bowl and cover with plastic wrap. Let the dough balls rest while making the Aloo Stuffing (potato mixture).

Aloo Stuffing

2	potatoes
5 sprigs	coriander
½ tsp	salt
½ tsp	garam masala
½ tsp	cumin seeds
¼ tsp	chilli flakes

1. Peel, chop and boil potatoes in a saucepan until soft and tender under a medium to high heat.

2. Drain and mash potatoes in a large bowl until smooth.

3. Chop the coriander and add to mashed potatoes.

4. Mix in remaining ingredients.

5. Make 8 balls roughly the same size as the dough balls.

Assembling the Aloo Paratha

1. Heat 1 tbs oil in a frying pan over medium heat.

2. Coat a dough ball in flour and flatten into a disc.

3. Roll out the dough disc, using a rolling pin, on a lightly floured surface, making it large enough to cover the potato ball.

4. Wrap potato ball with the dough disc. Gathering the edges, pinch together to seal and flatten into a disc again.

5. Coat all sides in flour, roll out the disc into a circle roughly 3mm (⅛ inch) thick.

6. Place the Paratha on heated pan. The dough will begin to change colour, and may puff up.

7. Flip over once the Paratha starts to brown underneath.

8. Lightly oil the cooked side of the Paratha. The Paratha should be finished cooking in 1–2 minutes. Oil second side once cooked.

➤ *Serve with pickle and fresh yoghurt.*

Soups & Stews

Autumn Minestrone Soup

Serves 8–10

1	onion
1 clove	garlic
1 stick	celery
140g (5 oz)	butternut squash
140g (5 oz)	potatoes
140g (5 oz)	cabbage
3 tbs	olive oil
1 can (400g/14 oz)	canned chopped tomatoes
2 litres (3 pints 9½ fl oz)	vegetable stock
310g (11 oz)	conchiglie pasta
2 tsp	dried oregano or basil
	salt and pepper to taste

Method

1. Finely chop onion, garlic and celery. Peel and chop butternut squash and potatoes and finely slice cabbage. Set aside.

2. Heat oil in a large saucepan. Add onion and garlic and sauté for 10 minutes or until lightly browned over medium heat.

3. Peel and chop butternut squash, potatoes and celery into small pieces and add to the sautéed onions.

4. Add butternut squash, potato. Mix well, then cover and cook for 10 minutes over a low heat.

5. Stir in canned tomatoes and simmer for 5 minutes.

6. Add cabbage and vegetable stock to the saucepan and bring to a boil.

7. Add conchiglie, cover and simmer until the pasta is cooked al dente.

8. Stir in basil or oregano. Add salt and pepper to taste.

Hearty Vegetable Soup

Lf

60g (2 oz)	onions
3 cloves	garlic
110g (4 oz)	celery
110g (4 oz)	leek
60g (2 oz)	sweet potato
170g (6 oz)	butternut squash
110g (4 oz)	carrots
2 tbs	olive oil
1 litre (1 pint 15 fl oz)	vegetable stock
	salt and pepper to taste

Method

1. Finely chop onion and garlic. Peel and chop the celery, leek, sweet potato, butternut squash and carrots into small chunks. Set aside.

2. Heat oil in a large pot. Add onion and garlic and sauté for 5 minutes or until translucent over medium heat.

3. Add vegetables and sauté for a further 5 minutes.

4. Add vegetable stock and bring to a slow boil.

5. Reduce heat and simmer for an additional 15–20 minutes or until all the vegetables are tender.

6. Liquidise ⅓ of the soup in a blender or food processor. Mix the purée into the rest of the soup and heat through. Add salt and pepper to taste.

➤ *Serve with a little crème fraiche and chopped parsley.*

Vegetable & Dumpling Stew

Dumplings

200g (7 oz)	self-raising flour
100g (4 oz)	butter
pinch	salt
pinch	pepper

1. Put flour into a mixing bowl and coarsely grate cold butter into the flour.

2. Add a pinch of salt and pepper. Mix the butter into the flour with fingertips until it resembles breadcrumbs.

3. Bring the mixture together and form a dough. Add some cold water if needed.

4. Divide the dough into 12 pieces. Roll each piece into a ball and set aside.

➤ *These dumplings can be used in any soup or stew.*

Stew

1	aubergine
1	onion
2 cloves	garlic
1 stick	celery
1	leek
2	carrots
1	red or yellow pepper
2	courgettes
3 tbs	olive oil
1 can (400g/14 oz)	canned tomatoes
500ml (17½ fl oz)	vegetable stock
1 tsp	ground cumin
small handful	fresh sage
300ml (10½ fl oz)	water
	salt and pepper to taste

1. Cut aubergine into cubes and sprinkle with salt. Leave for 20 minutes then pat dry.

2. Finely chop onion, garlic and celery. Slice leeks and peppers into rounds, Chop courgettes into semi-circles, peel and dice carrots, and slice the pepper. Sauté over a low heat in a large saucepan with oil.

3. Heat oil in a large saucepan. Add onion and garlic and sauté for 5 minutes or until translucent over medium heat.

4. Add celery and leeks and sauté for 2 minutes on medium heat.

5. Add carrots, pepper, courgettes and aubergine then cover and cook for 5 minutes, stirring occasionally.

6. Liquidise tomatoes. Add tomatoes and vegetable stock to the saucepan and stir well.

7. Add cumin, chopped sage and add salt and pepper to taste. Stir well.

8. Add the dumplings and water. Cover the pan and cook over a low heat for 20–25 minutes.

Leek & Potato Soup

Gf

1	onion
1 clove	garlic
455g (1 lb)	potatoes
2	leeks
30g (1 oz)	butter
1 litre (1 pint 15 fl oz)	vegetable stock
1 sprig (or 1 tbs if dry)	fresh thyme
100ml (3½ fl oz)	double cream
	salt and pepper to taste

Method

1. Finely slice onions and chop garlic. Peel and chop potatoes into cubes and slice leeks into thin rounds.

2. Melt butter in a saucepan, add onion and garlic and sauté for 5 minutes or until translucent over medium heat.

3. Add potatoes and leeks and sauté for 2–3 minutes.

4. Add the vegetable stock and bring to a boil over high heat. Cover and reduce to simmer until the potatoes and leeks are tender.

5. Add thyme (chopped if fresh) and add salt and pepper to taste.

6. Remove from the heat and pour in double cream. Mix well then liquidise with blender or food processor until smooth.

7. Return to heat and gently warm to serve.

➤ *Serve hot with soft cheese and rustic bread drizzled with extra virgin olive oil.*

French Onion Soup

30g (1 oz)	butter
6	onions
750ml (1 pint 6 fl oz)	vegetable stock
1	bay leaf
1 sprig	fresh parsley
1 sprig	fresh thyme
1 tsp	yeast extract
1 tsp	wholemeal flour
4–6 slices	bread
140–170g (5–6 oz)	cheddar cheese
	salt and pepper to taste
	sugar to taste

Method

1. Slice onions. Melt butter in a saucepan, add onion and sauté for 5 minutes or until translucent over medium heat.

2. Add vegetable stock, bay leaf, parsley, thyme and yeast extract and simmer for 10–15 minutes.

3. Mix flour with a little water in a bowl ensuring there are no lumps. Add to the saucepan and simmer for 10 minutes or until mixture thickens.

4. Remove the bay leaf and discard. Add sugar, salt and pepper to taste.

5. Toast bread, sprinkle on grated cheese and place on a baking tray. Grill for 2-3 minutes or until the cheese has melted and is golden and bubbly.

6. Serve soup in bowls with cheese toast on top.

Roasted Tomato & Basil Soup

1	red onion
2 cloves	garlic
590g (1 lb 5oz)	cherry or small tomatoes
2 tbs	extra virgin olive oil
1 tsp	balsamic vinegar
500ml (17½ fl oz)	vegetable stock
30g (1 oz)	fresh basil
	salt and pepper to taste

Preheat oven to 180°C/350°F/Gas 4

Method

1. Slice onion and crush garlic. Put in a roasting tin with tomatoes and add salt and pepper to taste.

2. Drizzle with oil and balsamic vinegar, then roast for 30 minutes.

3. Liquidise roasted ingredients and vegetable stock with a blender.

4. Add salt and pepper to taste and sprinkle basil leaves on top.

➤ *Serve with a spoon of sour cream and crusty bread.*

Spicy Carrot Soup

2 cloves	garlic
3 tbs	olive oil
3 tsp	ground cumin
I tsp	ground cayenne pepper
I	onion
I	celery
4	carrots
2	potatoes
I litre (I pint I5 fl oz)	vegetable stock
	salt to taste

Method

1. Crush garlic, finely chop onions and celery and peel and chop potatoes and carrots.

2. Heat oil in a large saucepan, add garlic, cumin, cayenne pepper, onions and celery and sauté for 3 minutes over low heat.

3. Add potatoes, carrots and vegetable stock and then bring to boil, and simmer for 30 minutes.

4. Add salt to taste and liquidise in a blender.

➤ Serve topped with chopped coriander leaves.

Celery & Cashew Soup

Gf Lf V

Serves 6–8

1 bunch (6 or 7 sticks)	celery, with leaves
2	onions
2 tbs	olive oil
2	potatoes
1½ litres (2 Pints 12 fl oz)	vegetable stock
500g (1 lb 2oz)	cashew nuts
2 tbs	fresh parsley
	salt and pepper to taste

Method

1. Wash and coarsely chop celery, including leaves. Peel onions and finely slice.

2. Heat oil in a large saucepan and add the celery and onions. Sauté for a few minutes or until the onion is tender and transparent over low heat.

3. Peel potatoes and dice into chunky cubes, add to the saucepan and heat through for a few minutes.

4. Increase heat to high and stir to avoid sticking to the pan. When the ingredients start to stick, add vegetable stock. Bring to boil then reduce heat to low. Cover and simmer for 10 minutes.

5. Wash cashew nuts, add to the saucepan and simmer for 20 minutes.

6. Remove the saucepan from the heat and add parsley and salt and pepper to taste. Allow the soup to cool a little then blend to desired consistency.

Cheese & Broccoli Soup

Serves 4

2	potatoes
1½ litres (2 Pints 12 fl oz)	water
1	onion
455g (1 lb)	broccoli
2 tbs	double cream
55g (2 oz)	blue cheese

Method

1. Peel and chop potatoes into chunks. Place in a pot of salted water and bring to boil.

2. Reduce heat to medium and cook for 5 minutes until the potatoes have softened and are almost cooked.

3. Chop onions and broccoli and add to the water. Cook for a further 5 minutes or until the vegetables are tender and cooked through.

4. Remove from heat and liquidize the mixture until smooth.

5. Mix in double cream and grated blue cheese and return to a low heat until the cheese has melted and the soup has warmed.

Ratatouille

1	onion
2 cloves	garlic
2	aubergines
6	tomatoes
220g (8 oz)	courgettes
1	yellow or red pepper
4 tbs	olive oil
½ tsp	salt
½ tsp	dried basil
½ tsp	dried oregano

Method

1. Finely slice aubergines, spread the slices on a plate and sprinkle with salt. Leave to stand for 20 minutes to allow the aubergines to release their bitter juice. Wash off all the salt and dry with a paper or tea towel. Chop into small chunks and set aside.

2. Place tomatoes in a large bowl and pour boiling water over them. Leave for 30 seconds or until the skin starts to blister. Drain the tomatoes, rinse under cold water and then remove skin. Chop the tomatoes and set aside.

3. Slice onion and crush garlic. Heat oil in a frying pan, add onion and garlic and sauté for 5 minutes or until lightly brown over medium heat.

4. Add tomatoes. Remove from heat and set aside.

5. In a separate frying pan, lightly fry aubergines, regularly turning them to cook evenly. When lightly browned all over (but still slightly firm) add to the fried onions and tomato mixture and set aside.

6. Slice the courgettes. Lightly sauté the courgettes in a frying pan over medium heat for a few minutes leaving them slightly firm. Add to the vegetable mixture.

7. Chop the pepper and sauté until cooked to the same degree as the aubergine and courgettes. Once cooked add to the rest of the vegetable mixture.

8. Return the vegetable and tomato mixture to a high heat and mix well.

9. Add salt, basil and oregano and simmer for 20–30 minutes. The vegetables should all be cooked and the tomatoes should have broken down to form a stew.

➤ *Serve hot with brown rice.*

Mushroom & Tarragon Soup

Serves 6

I	onion
I clove	garlic
60g (2 oz)	butter
340g (12 oz)	field or chestnut mushrooms
I tbs	dried tarragon
500ml (17½ fl oz)	vegetable stock
250ml (9 fl oz)	milk
150ml (5½ fl oz)	single cream
	salt and pepper to taste

Method

1. Finely chop onion and crush garlic. Melt butter in a saucepan; add the onion and garlic and sauté for 5 minutes or until soft and transparent over medium heat.

2. Add sliced mushrooms and dried tarragon to the saucepan; turn up the heat to medium and cook for 10 minutes until the mushrooms are soft.

3. Add vegetable stock and bring to boil before simmering for 15–20 minutes.

4. Remove from heat, add milk and salt and pepper to taste, then liquidise. Return to heat and gently warm.

5. Add single cream.

Chilli Bean Stew

225g (8 oz)	onion
I clove	garlic
75g (3 oz)	celery
75g (3 oz)	green pepper
75g (3 oz)	carrot
I tbs	olive oil
I can (400g/14 oz)	canned red kidney beans
½ tsp	dried basil
½ tsp	ground cumin
¼ tsp	ground cayenne pepper
I can (400g/14 oz)	canned tomatoes
2 tbs	tomato purée
3 tbs	red wine vinegar
I tbs	dark brown sugar
60g (2 oz)	bulgur wheat
570ml (I pint)	vegetable stock
I	lemon
	salt and pepper to taste

Method

1. Finely chop onion, garlic, celery, green pepper and carrots. Set aside.

2. Heat oil in a large saucepan, add onions and garlic and sauté for 5 minutes or until the onions are soft and transparent over medium heat.

3. Add the celery, green pepper and carrots to the saucepan.

4. Drain and wash the canned red kidney beans and add along with basil and spices to the vegetable mixture. Stir and cook for 5 minutes over a high heat.

5. Liquidise the canned tomatoes and add along with tomato purée, vinegar, sugar, bulgur wheat and vegetable stock to the saucepan. Bring to boil, cover and simmer for 30 minutes. The bulgur wheat will soak up most of the stock making the stew thick, so add extra stock if necessary or desired.

6. Add lemon juice and salt and pepper to taste.

➤ *Serve hot with green salad and natural yoghurt. Can also be served with grated cheddar.*

Chilli Bean & Soya Stew

At step 5, Replace bulgur wheat with soya chunks 60g (2oz). Wash and drain soya chunks. Add to stew instead of bulgur wheat along with an extra 570ml (1 pint) of vegetable stock.

Chilli Bean & Butternut Squash Stew

At step 5, Add butternut squash, peeled and chopped into bite size chunks, with an extra 570ml (1 pint) of vegetable stock. The butternut squash should be tender when ready.

Beetroot & Thyme Soup

Serves 4

1	onion
1	carrot
1	sweet potato
4–5	beetroot
2 cloves	garlic
3 tbs	olive oil
1 sprig	fresh thyme
1½ litres (2 pints 12 fl oz)	vegetable stock
½ tsp	ground cumin
	salt and pepper to taste

Method

1. Dice onions and carrots, peel and chop sweet potato and beetroot into small chunks and peel and crush garlic. Set aside.

2. Heat oil in a large saucepan, add onions and carrots and sauté for 5 minutes or until onions are soft and translucent over medium heat.

3. Add garlic, sweet potato, beetroot and thyme to the saucepan. Mix well.

4. Add vegetable stock and ground cumin. Bring to boil, cover and simmer for 20 minutes or until the vegetables are tender.

5. Remove the mixture from the heat and liquidise until smooth.

6. Reheat soup over a low to medium heat and add salt and pepper to taste.

➤ *Serve with crème fraîche or sour cream.*

Spiced Butternut Squash Soup

Serves 4

Gf

1kg (2 lb 4 oz)	butternut squash
2	onions
2 cloves	garlic
60g (2 oz)	butter
2 tsp	ground cumin
1 litre (1 pint 15 fl oz)	vegetable stock
110ml (4 fl oz)	double cream

Method

1. Cut butternut squash in half, peel outer skin, de-seed core and chop into 2½cm (1 inch) pieces. Chop onions and garlic. Set aside.

2. Heat butter in a large saucepan. Add onions, garlic and butternut squash and sauté covered for 5 minutes on low heat, stirring occasionally.

3. Add ground cumin and vegetable stock and bring the soup to boil then reduce to low heat and cover. Simmer for 15 minutes until the squash is tender.

4. Once tender, remove from heat and add double cream.

5. Liquidise the soup until smooth and return to heat to warm.

➤ *Serve with finely chopped coriander.*

Watercress Soup

I	onion
I	potato
I tbs	olive oil
750ml (I pint 6 fl oz)	vegetable stock
200g (7 oz)	fresh watercress

Method

1. Peel and coarsely chop onion and potato. Set aside.

2. Heat oil in a large saucepan, add onion and sauté over medium heat for 5 minutes or until soft and transparent.

3. Add the potato and sauté for approximately 2–3 minutes.

4. Add vegetable stock and watercress. Bring to boil then simmer for 15 minutes or until all the ingredients are soft.

5. Once soft remove from heat and liquidise until smooth. Then return to heat to warm.

Vegetable Stock

Gf Lf V

Makes 1 ¼ litres (2 pints 3½ fl oz)

2	bay leaves
1	carrot
1	parsnip
2	onions
6 sticks	celery
1 tsp	black peppercorns
3 litres (5 pints 4½ fl oz)	water

Method

1. Peel and chop vegetables.

2. Place all ingredients in a large saucepan. Bring to a boil then simmer uncovered for 1½ hours.

3. Remove from the heat and strain, discarding the vegetables and spices. The stock can be used for soups, stew and gravy and can be frozen for up to 6 months.

Gazpacho

Serves 4

400g (14 oz)	tomatoes
1	onion
1 clove	garlic
2	spring onions
1	green pepper
1	cucumber
½	lemon
1	lime
1 litre (1 pint 15 fl oz)	tomato juice
1 tsp	dried basil
60g (2 oz)	fresh parsley
1 tsp	honey
2 tbs	wine vinegar
2 tbs	olive oil
1 tsp	dried tarragon
1 tsp	Tabasco or hot sauce
1 tsp	ground cumin
	salt and pepper to taste

Method

1. Place tomatoes in a large bowl and cover with boiling water. Leave for 30 seconds or until the skin starts to blister. Drain tomatoes, rinse under cold water then remove skin and dice. Place in a bowl and set aside.

2. Finely chop onion and garlic and add to the bowl.

3. Finely dice spring onions, green pepper and cucumber to a uniform size and add to the tomatoes and onions.

4. Squeeze lemon and lime and pour juice into the bowl.

5. Pour in tomato juice and follow with the rest of the ingredients. Mix well and allow to chill in a fridge for 2 hours before serving. The soup can be blended or partially blended if preferred; however, it is traditionally served chunky.

➤ *Serve cold.*

Hot & Sour Bean Curd & Noodle Soup

Serves 4

Lf V

Stock

2	red chillies
1½cm (½ inch)	ginger
½ stalk	lemongrass
1	onion
1	lemon
1½ litres (2 pints 12 fl oz)	water
80ml (3 fl oz)	light soy sauce
	salt to taste

1. Chop red chillies, ginger, lemongrass and onion. Place in a saucepan and set aside.

2. Squeeze the juice from the lemon and add to the pan.

3. Add water to the pan along with all the fresh stock ingredients. Bring to boil and simmer for 5 minutes.

4. Strain the stock into a container and discard the ingredients. Return the stock to the pan and add light soy sauce and salt.

Soup

250g (9 oz)	tofu
80g (3 oz)	mushrooms
250g (9 oz)	thick rice noodles (soup noodles)
110g (4 oz)	fresh watercress or coriander
	oil for frying

1. Pour enough oil into a frying pan to cover the base.

2. Slice tofu in rectangular pieces approximately 1cm x 2.5cm (½ inch x1 inch). Fry the tofu for 2 minutes, turning regularly to brown evenly.

3. Remove tofu from the oil and add to the stock. Return the stock to a high heat and bring to boil.

4. Add finely sliced mushrooms and noodles to the stock. Boil for a further 3 minutes.

5. Add watercress or coriander to the stock and continue to boil until the noodles are cooked.

➤ *Serve hot with dark soy sauce or tamari..*

Pea & Mint Soup

Serves 4

60g (2 oz)	butter
450g (1 lb)	peas (fresh or frozen)
500ml (17½ fl oz)	vegetable stock
small handful	fresh mint
	salt and pepper to taste

Method

1. Place a large saucepan over a medium low heat and add butter.

2. If using fresh peas, shell and wash them. Add peas to saucepan. Cover the saucepan and cook for 10 minutes, occasionally stirring.

3. Add vegetable stock, bring to boil then cover and simmer for 20 minutes.

4. Remove the pan from the heat, add finely chopped mint and blend soup until completely smooth. Add salt and pepper to taste.

➤ *Serve with single cream and sprigs of mint.*

Delicate Tomato Soup

500ml (17½ fl oz)	water
1	onion
1 stick	celery
½	apple
1	beetroot
680g (1 lb 8 oz)	tomatoes
	salt and pepper to taste

Method

1. Place water in a pan and bring to boil.

2. Coarsely chop onion, celery, apple and beetroot. Place the ingredients into the pan of boiling water, reduce heat to low and simmer for 10 minutes.

3. Place tomatoes in a large bowl and cover with boiling water. Leave for 30 seconds or until the skin starts to blister. Drain tomatoes, rinse under cold water then remove skin.

4. Chop tomatoes into chunks and add to the pan of vegetables. Remove from heat and blend mixture until smooth.

5. Add salt and pepper to taste. Pour the mixture back in the pan and continue to heat until warmed.

➤ *Serve topped with chopped parsley and lemon thyme. Can be served cold.*

Irish Stew with Seitan

Serves 4–5

2 tbs	olive oil
I	onions
I stalks	celery
4	potatoes
375g (13 oz)	baby carrots
½	leek
2 cloves	garlic
I	bay leaves
80g (3 oz)	pearl barley
750 litres (I pints 6 fl oz)	vegetable stock
170g (6 oz)	seitan (wheat gluten)
50ml (2 fl oz)	soy sauce
170g (6 oz)	button mushroom
60g (2 oz)	kale
I tsp	dried thyme
	salt and pepper to taste

Method

1. Heat oil in a large pot over a medium heat. Chop onions and celery into medium size pieces, add to the pot and cook with the lid on for about 5 minutes, or until soft.

2. Peel potatoes and cube into 2cm (I inch) pieces. Peel carrots and slice into 1½cm (½ inch) rounds. Slice leek lengthwise and chop into 1½cm (½ inch) chunks. Crush garlic, then add ingredients to the pot, with bay leaves, and allow to fry for 2 minutes.

3. Add barley and vegetable stock, bring to a boil then reduce to a low heat and simmer for 15 minutes.

4. Chop seitan into bite size pieces. Fry in a small pan with some olive oil until browned, over a medium heat.

5. Finely chop kale and slice mushrooms into halves, add to the pot with seitan, soy sauce and thyme. Increase to a high heat until the stew bubbles slightly then reduce heat to simmer for 10–15 minutes. Add salt and pepper to taste.

Irish Stew with Tofu

170g (6oz)	firm tofu
50ml (2 fl oz)	soy sauce
	salt and pepper to taste

At step 4, replace seitan with tofu. Fry in a small pan with olive oil until golden. Add soy sauce and salt and pepper to taste.

Irish Stew with Soya Chunks

At step 4, replace seitan with equal amounts of soya chunks.
Soak soya chunks in hot water until soft and doubled in size. Drain and squeeze out any water from soya chunks then fry in small pan with some olive oil until browned, over medium heat.

Salads & Dressings

Carrot & Beetroot Salad with Toasted Seeds

Serves 4

300g (11 oz)	beetroot
220g (8 oz)	carrots
140g (5 oz)	apples
110g (4 oz)	celery
3 leaves	red cabbage
small handful	parsley
80g (3 oz)	pumpkin seeds
2	oranges
3 tbs	olive oil
1 tsp	ground cumin
	salt and pepper to taste

Method

1. Peel beetroot and carrots and core apples. Coarsely grate ingredients into a large salad bowl.

2. Finely slice celery and shred cabbage leaves and chop parsley, then add to the salad bowl.

3. Heat the olive oil in a frying pan over a medium heat and lightly roast pumpkin seeds. Add immediately to the rest of the salad.

4. Juice oranges and pour juice into the bowl. Add olive oil, cumin, salt and pepper and mix until combined. Drizzle over the salad and toss.

Avocado, Couscous & Tomato Salad

Serves 4

200g (7 oz)	couscous
300ml (11 fl oz)	vegetable stock
2	avocados
110g (4 oz)	canned chickpeas
140g (5 oz)	cherry tomatoes
140g (5 oz)	mozzarella cheese
1 tbs	lemon juice
	salt and pepper to taste
	olive oil as required

Method

1. Add couscous into a salad bowl.

2. Heat the vegetable stock and pour over the couscous and cover. Leave to stand for 5 minutes or until the water from the stock is absorbed.

3. Fluff up the couscous with a fork. Drizzle with olive oil and toss.

4. Drain and rinse chickpeas in a sieve. Peel avocadoes and slice into medium sized pieces. Halve cherry tomatoes and tear mozzarella into small pieces. Add to the couscous.

5. Squeeze lemon juice over the salad and add salt and pepper to taste. Gently toss again, taking care not to break up the avocadoes.

Black Bean & Brown Rice Salad

250g (9 oz)	dried or canned black beans
500g (1 lb 2 oz)	brown rice
500g (1 lb 2 oz)	cherry tomatoes
1	yellow pepper
½	red onion
4 cloves	garlic
1	lemon
1 tbs	dried basil
1 tsp	dried oregano
½ tsp	ground paprika
1 tbs	salt
½ tbs	black pepper
½	cucumber
	olive oil as required

Preheat oven to 200°C/400°F/Gas 6

Method

1. If using canned beans skip to step 3. If using dried beans, soak them until they have doubled in size, approximately 4 hours or leave overnight. Put in a pressure cooker, cover with water and cook for 15–20 minutes over a medium heat.

2. Drain beans in a sieve and rinse with cold water.

3. Wash brown rice thoroughly and place in a saucepan of boiling water. Bring to a boil, then reduce heat and simmer for 20 minutes or until cooked.

4. Quarter cherry tomatoes, cube yellow pepper and finely dice red onion. Place in a deep baking tray along with the cooked black beans.

5. Juice the lemon and add to the baking tray with basil, oregano, paprika, salt, black pepper, crushed garlic and a little olive oil. Mix well then place in the oven for 20 minutes, removing to stir occasionally.

6. Drain rice in a sieve, rinse with cold water, then pour boiling water evenly over and return to a large pan. Add a little olive oil, stir and cover.

7. Dice cucumber and add to rice. Mix in the vegetables and beans. Add extra salt and pepper to taste.

➤ *Serve warm, or refrigerate and serve cold. (Also great with marinated tofu.)*

Chickpea Salad

150g (5oz)	couscous
300ml (11 floz)	vegetable stock
200g (7oz)	canned chickpeas
110g (4oz)	sun-dried tomatoes
150g (5oz)	feta cheese
30g (1oz)	pine nuts
1	lemon
1 bunch	fresh mint
	olive oil as required
	salt and pepper to taste

Method

1. Heat the vegetable stock and pour over the couscous. Cover and leave to stand for 5 minutes. Once water from stock has been absorbed, fluff up the couscous with a fork.

2. Drain and rinse chickpeas then add to the couscous.

3. Roughly chop sun-dried tomatoes and crumble feta into small pieces. Add to bowl.

4. Toast pine nuts in a small frying pan until lightly golden, over a medium heat. Toss frequently, as they brown easily. Sprinkle into the bowl.

5. Squeeze the lemon, then drizzle lemon juice and olive oil over the couscous and chickpeas. Finely chop mint and fold it in carefully. Add salt and pepper to taste.

➤ Can be served with a side of plain yoghurt.

Toasted Halloumi & Pine Nut Salad

Serves 4

2 tbs	pine nuts
2	red onions
60g (2 oz)	rocket leaves
4 tbs	capers
12	baby plum tomatoes
small handful	fresh tarragon
small handful	fresh parsley
3 tbs	olive oil
2 tsp	lemon juice
250g (9 oz)	halloumi cheese
	black pepper to taste

Method

1. Toast pine nuts in a frying pan over a medium heat, tossing lightly until golden, then set aside.

2. Peel and slice red onions into rings. Place in a large bowl.

3. Add rocket and capers to the bowl. Halve tomatoes and scatter on top.

4. Finely chop tarragon and parsley. Add to the salad with olive oil and lemon juice. Grind some black pepper evenly over, toss gently and pile onto 4 plates.

5. Cut halloumi into 8 slices, then halve each slice lengthways. Place on aluminium foil and grill on one side only for 3 minutes, or until lightly golden.

6. Divide the halloumi between the plates. Scatter the pine nuts on top.

➤ *Serve with crusty bread.*

Roast Pear, Hazelnut & Blue Cheese Salad

Gf

Serves 4

1	red onion
3	pears
30g (1 oz)	unsalted butter
140g (5 oz)	rocket, watercress and spinach leaves
80g (3 oz)	hazelnuts
170g (6 oz)	mild blue cheese
	olive oil as required

Dressing

2½ tsp	white wine vinegar
½ tsp	Dijon mustard
4 tbs	hazelnut oil
2 tbs	light olive oil
1 tsp	caster sugar
	salt and pepper to taste

Preheat oven to 180°C/350°F/Gas 4

Method

1. Slice onion into long, thin pieces. Place in a small ovenproof dish, drizzle with olive oil and season with salt and pepper. Roast for 20–30 minutes.

2. For the dressing, place ingredients in a large salad bowl, mix thoroughly with a whisk or fork and add salt and pepper to taste. Remove ¼ of the dressing and set aside.

3. Halve and core pears, then slice into long pieces ½cm (¼ inch) thick.

4. Melt butter in a frying pan then sauté the pear slices on each side over a low to medium heat, until golden.

5. Halve hazelnuts and toast lightly in a small frying pan over a medium heat. Put in a large bowl with the salad leaves. Drizzle with the dressing and toss gently. Arrange in mounds on 4 plates.

6. Add the pears and onion to each mound and crumble the cheese evenly on top. Drizzle with the rest of the dressing.

UK Potato Salad

Serves 4

900g (2 lb)	new potatoes
3	spring onions
5	green olives
I bunch	chives
I	gherkin
2 tbs	lemon juice
	salt and pepper to taste

Mayonnaise

125ml (4½ fl oz)	soya milk
I tsp	Dijon mustard
½ tsp	cider vinegar
200ml (7 fl oz)	vegetable oil
	salt to taste

Method

1. For the mayonnaise, mix soya milk, mustard and vinegar in a blender at high speed. Slowly pour in vegetable oil, blending between additions until the mixture is thick and creamy. Add a little extra oil if needed and season with salt.

2. Wash and scrub potatoes, then cut into quarters and place in boiling water. Cook for 8–10 minutes until softened but still a little firm. Rinse with cold water and set aside.

3. Finely slice spring onions, green olives, chives and gherkin. Place in a large salad bowl. Drizzle with lemon juice and mix well.

4. Put the mayonnaise in the bowl and mix with the other ingredients. Add the potatoes and gently combine, taking care not to break up the potatoes. Add salt to taste.

Pasta Salad

Serves 4

310g (11 oz)	conchiglie pasta
250g (9 oz)	yellow cherry tomatoes
250g (9 oz)	red cherry tomatoes
60g (2 oz)	black olives
2 tbs	fresh chives
30g (1 oz)	fresh basil
200g (7 oz)	cucumber

Dressing

3 cloves	garlic
4 tbs	white wine vinegar
100ml (3½ fl oz)	olive oil
	salt and pepper to taste

Method

1. Bring a large pan of salted water to boil. Place pasta shells and unpeeled cloves of garlic into the pan and boil until pasta is cooked al dente.

2. Drain pasta under cold water and place into a salad bowl. Keep the garlic aside for dressing.

3. Halve the tomatoes and olives. Dice cucumber and finely chop basil and chives, then add to the salad bowl.

4. To make the dressing, crush garlic using a pestle and mortar. Add vinegar, olive oil and seasoning and mix until well blended.

5. Drizzle the dressing over the salad and toss till evenly coated.

Sweet Potato & Green Bean Salad

150g (5 oz)	green beans
2	sweet potatoes
2 cloves	garlic
1 tbs	fresh thyme
1	red gem lettuce
100g (4 oz)	baby spinach
100g (4 oz)	rocket
150g (5 oz)	cherry tomatoes
2	spring onions
1	yellow pepper
2	avocadoes
	olive oil as required
	salt and pepper to taste

Preheat oven to 220°C/425°F/Gas 7

Method

1. Trim ends off green beans and wash. Place in a saucepan of boiling water and cook for 3-4 minutes, until al dente. Drain and set aside.

2. Peel, wash and slice sweet potatoes into 1cm (½ inch) rounds. Place in a saucepan of boiling water and parboil for 5 minutes. Drain, and place on a baking tray.

3. Drizzle sweet potato with olive oil. Sprinkle evenly with crushed garlic and finely chopped thyme. Add salt and pepper and roast in the oven for 10 minutes, until slightly crispy and aromatic.

4. Roughly chop lettuce, spinach and rocket leaves and place in a large bowl.

5. Halve tomatoes, finely chop spring onions and cube yellow pepper. Cut avocado in half, remove seed, remove skin and slice. Add to the bowl with green beans and sweet potato and toss well.

➤ *Drizzle with olive oil and balsamic vinegar to serve.*

Quinoa & Broad Bean Salad

Serves 4

100g (4oz)	fresh or frozen broad beans
2 tsp	salt
200g (7oz)	quinoa
100g (4oz)	frozen peas
60g (2oz)	flaked almonds
50ml (2 floz)	olive oil
1	lemon
200g (7oz)	feta cheese
small bunch	fresh mint
small bunch	fresh dill

Method

1. Place broad beans in a saucepan of boiling water and cook for 3–4 minutes, taking care to remove from the heat before they change colour. Drain and put in a bowl of cold water.

2. Place quinoa and 1 tsp of salt in a saucepan with 400ml of boiling water. Bring to a boil, reduce to a low heat and simmer for 10 minutes, or until the water has been absorbed by the quinoa. Remove from heat, cover, and set aside for 30 minutes.

3. Peel the outer skins off the broad beans and discard, and put the beans into a large salad bowl.

4. Place peas in a saucepan of boiling water and cook for a few minutes. Drain in a sieve under cold running water and add to the salad bowl.

5. Toast the almonds in a frying pan for a few minutes over a medium to high heat. Turn occasionally until golden then set aside.

6. Add quinoa to broad beans and peas.

7. Juice lemon, finely chop mint and dill, crumble feta and add to the bowl. Pour in oil and sprinkle with flaked almonds. Mix until all ingredients are evenly combined then serve.

Coleslaw

6 leaves	green cabbage
3 leaves	red cabbage
60g (2 oz)	carrots

Dressing

I	red onion
50ml (2 fl oz)	plain yoghurt
225ml (8 fl oz)	honey
I tbs	mustard
I tsp	milk
I tsp	lemon juice
¼ tsp	sugar
½ tsp	celery seeds
I tsp	dried parsley
	salt and pepper to taste

Method

1. Wash cabbage leaves and divide each down the centre, then shred finely. Wash, peel and coarsely grate carrots. Put together in a large salad bowl.

2. For the dressing, finely dice red onion and place in a medium sized bowl. Add other ingredients and beat with a whisk or fork until thoroughly combined. Add salt and pepper to taste.

3. Pour the dressing over the cabbage and carrots and mix well.

Greek Salad

Serves 2

1	cos lettuce
½	cucumber
4	tomatoes
2	spring onions
handful	black olives
110g (4 oz)	feta cheese

Dressing

90ml (3 fl oz)	white wine vinegar
150ml (5 fl oz)	olive oil
	salt and pepper to taste

Method

1. Slice lettuce into 1cm (½ inch) thick strips. Quarter cucumber lengthways and cut into 1cm (½ inch) chunks. Place in a large salad bowl.

2. Cut tomatoes into thin wedges. Chop spring onions into small pieces and toss into the bowl. Add olives to the bowl.

3. Cut feta into small cubes and sprinkle gently into the bowl.

4. For the dressing, beat vinegar together with salt and pepper in a small bowl using a whisk or fork. Gradually add oil and whisk until smooth.

5. Pour over the salad and toss.

Summer Salad Dressing

110g (4oz)	yoghurt
½ tbs	mustard
2 tbs	honey
1 tsp	milk
1 tsp	lemon juice
½ tsp	sugar
1	red onion
½ tsp	celery seed
1 tsp	dried parsley
	salt and pepper to taste

Method

1. Mix yoghurt, mustard and honey thoroughly in a large bowl, with a whisk or fork.

2. Add milk, lemon juice and sugar then mix until the ingredients emulsify.

3. Grate onion into the bowl. Add celery seed and parsley.

4. Add salt and pepper to taste and mix to an even texture.

Herb & Spice Dressing

1	shallot
1 clove	garlic
2 tbs	cider vinegar
2 leaves	fresh basil
1 tbs	fresh mint
pinch	salt
pinch	chilli powder
pinch	ground cayenne pepper

Method

1. Finely chop shallot and garlic and place in a small bowl.

2. Add cider vinegar and set aside for a few minutes to reduce the pungency of the shallot.

3. Finely chop basil and mint and add to the bowl.

4. Sprinkle with salt, chilli powder and cayenne pepper. Mix to an even texture and set aside to marinate.

Yoghurt Dressing

110g (4oz)	yoghurt
1 tsp	ground cumin
2 tsp	honey
2 tbs	lemon juice
1 clove	garlic
	salt and pepper to taste

Method

1. Mix yoghurt, cumin, honey and lemon juice thoroughly in a large bowl, with a whisk or fork.

2. Crush garlic and add to the bowl.

3. Mix to an even texture and serve immediately, or refrigerate until ready to serve.

French Dressing

1 tsp	caster sugar
1½ tsp	mustard powder
6 tbs	olive oil
4 tbs	cider vinegar
	salt and pepper to taste

Method

1. Mix sugar, mustard and olive oil thoroughly in a small bowl, with a whisk or fork.

2. Pour in vinegar and mix until the ingredients emulsify.

3. Add salt and pepper to taste and mix to an even texture.

Honey & Mustard Dressing

1 tbs	French mustard
1 tbs	honey
1 tsp	balsamic vinegar
2 tbs	cider vinegar
1 clove	garlic
6 tbs	sunflower oil
	salt and pepper to taste

Method

1. Blend French mustard, honey, balsamic vinegar and cider vinegar in a food processor.

2. Crush the garlic into the mixture and pour in the oil while blending at a low speed.

3. Add salt and pepper to taste and pulse to mix to an even texture.

Lemon & Basil Salad Dressing

6 tbs	extra virgin olive oil
2 tbs	lemon juice
6 leaves	fresh basil
	salt and pepper to taste

Method

1. Whisk olive oil and lemon juice in a small bowl until they reach a smooth consistency.

2. Finely chop or tear basil leaves into small pieces and add to the bowl.

3. Add salt and pepper to taste and mix to an even texture.

White Balsamic Dressing

6 tbs	olive oil
2 tbs	white balsamic vinegar
½ tbs	sugar
1 tbs	fresh parsley
	salt and pepper to taste

Method

1. Put oil, vinegar and sugar in a bowl and whisk until well combined.

2. Finely chop the parsley and add to the other ingredients.

3. Add salt and pepper to taste and mix well.

Hazelnut Dressing

2½ tsp	white wine vinegar
½ tsp	Dijon mustard
4 tbs	hazelnut oil
2 tbs	light olive oil
1 tsp	caster sugar
	salt and pepper to taste

Method

1. Mix ingredients thoroughly in a large salad bowl with a whisk or fork.

2. Add salt and pepper to taste and mix to an even texture.

Basic Vinaigrette

6 tbs	extra virgin olive oil
2 tbs	balsamic vinegar
2 tsp	mustard
	ground black pepper to taste

Method

1. Put all the ingredients in a jar, put on the lid and shake vigorously.

Mains

Lancashire Hot Pot

Filling

1	onion
1 clove	garlic
3	parsnips
3	carrots
5 stalks	celery
50ml (2 fl oz)	olive oil
2 tbs	tomato purée
3 tbs	pearl barley
450ml (16 fl oz)	vegetable stock
2 tbs	fresh thyme
	salt and pepper to taste

Preheat oven to 180°C/350°F/Gas 4

1. Slice onion and crush garlic. Chop parsnips, carrots and celery into 3cm (1 1/2 inch) pieces. Set aside.

2. Heat olive oil in a frying pan, add onion and garlic and sauté over medium heat for 5 minutes or until translucent.

3. Add tomato purée and cook for another 5 minutes, stirring often.

4. Add the parsnips, carrots, celery, and barley, vegetable stock, and thyme and stir. Simmer for 30 minutes or until vegetables and barley are tender. Add salt and pepper to taste.

5. Either divide the mixture evenly among 6 small ramekins or into 1 large pie dish.

Topping

4	baking potatoes
2 tbs	olive oil
	salt and pepper to taste

1. Peel and thinly slice potatoes and season with salt and pepper to taste. Arrange in an overlapping layer on top of the vegetable mixture in the ramekins or pie dish.

2. Brush with olive oil and bake for 30 minutes or until potatoes are brown.

Lancashire Hot Pot with Soya Mince
At step 4, add 200g (7 oz) of soya mince or crumbled firm tofu to the vegetables.

Mushroom Stroganoff

Serves 4

340g (12 oz)	button mushrooms
1	onion
4 sticks	celery
60g (2 oz)	unsalted butter
1 tbs	wholemeal flour
150ml (5½ fl oz)	water
1 tsp	vegetable stock powder
1	bay leaf
½ tsp	dried thyme
150ml (5½ fl oz)	sour cream
small handful	parsley
	salt and pepper to taste

Method

1. Clean mushrooms by wiping with a slightly damp cloth. Peel and finely slice onion. Chop celery into thin pieces.

2. Melt 30g (1 oz) of butter in a frying pan, add celery and onion and sauté over medium heat for 5 minutes or until translucent.

3. Melt remaining butter, then put in mushrooms and sauté for 2–3 minutes.

4. Mix flour and water in a small bowl to form a paste, adding water a little at a time to ensure it is smooth. Add paste to the mushrooms and mix well.

5. Sprinkle vegetable stock into the mixture. Add bay leaf and dried thyme, and bring to a boil. Reduce to low heat and simmer for a further 2–3 minutes.

6. Remove the frying pan from the heat and allow to cool slightly. Remove bay leaf, stir in sour cream and add salt and pepper to taste.

➤ *Garnish with chopped parsley and serve with brown rice and green vegetables.*

Pizza

Dough

220g (8 oz)	plain flour
½ tsp	salt
¼ tsp	caster sugar
I tsp	fast action dried yeast
I tbs	olive oil
150ml (5½ fl oz)	warm water
	olive oil for greasing and drizzling

1. Sift flour into a bowl. Add salt, sugar and yeast and mix well.

2. Create a well in the centre of the mixed dry ingredients, add oil and then slowly pour in warm waterMix the ingredients to form a soft dough.

3. Turn the dough out onto a lightly floured surface and knead for 5 minutes or until smooth and elastic.

4. Set aside the dough in a bowl, covered with cling film, in a draught free place for an hour or until doubled in size.

Sauce

4	tomatoes
3 tbs	tomato purée
½ tsp	caster sugar
	salt and pepper to taste

1. Put tomatoes in a large heatproof bowl. Cover with boiling water, leave to stand for 30 seconds or until the skin starts to split. Drain and pour over cold water.

2. Peel tomatoes and discard skin. Chop into chunks and put into a separate bowl. Add tomato purée, sugar, and salt and pepper to taste and mix well.

Topping

80g (3 oz)	mozzarella cheese
10 leaves	fresh basil

Preheat oven to 220°C/425°F/Gas 7

1. Place a large pizza tray/baking tray inside the oven to heat.

2. Re-knead the dough and on a lightly floured surface, roll out to a round of 30–35cm (12–14 inches).

3. Place the base onto the tray. Add sauce, cheese and drizzle with olive oil and then bake for 12–15 minutes or until the crust is slightly rolled, golden and crisp. Remove from oven and sprinkle with basil.

Spinach Cannelloni

Serves 4

Spinach Filling

280g (10 oz)	frozen spinach
30g (1 oz)	butter
140g (5 oz)	Italian hard cheese
2 cloves	garlic
310g (11 oz)	cottage cheese
1 tsp	dried dill
⅛ tsp	ground nutmeg
1 tsp	lemon juice
	salt and pepper to taste

1. Put spinach in a saucepan and allow to defrost over gentle heat. Drain any excess water and add butter.

2. Grate Italian hard cheese and crush garlic. Add hard cheese, garlic, cottage cheese, dill and nutmeg to the spinach.

3. Continue to simmer over gentle heat. Add lemon juice and add salt and pepper to taste. Add more nutmeg and lemon juice to taste.

Tomato Sauce

1	onion
2	garlic
2	courgettes
1 can (400g/14 oz)	canned tomatoes
2 tsp	balsamic vinegar
1 tbs	sugar
1 tsp	dried basil
	olive oil for frying

1. Finely chop onion. Heat olive oil in a saucepan, add onion and sauté over low heat for 5 minutes or until translucent.

2. Crush garlic and finely dice courgettes. Add to the saucepan and gently sauté on medium heat until courgettes soften. Take care not to apply too much heat as the garlic may burn.

3. Blend the tomatoes, add to the saucepan and stir well. Increase to high heat

until the mixture starts to boil, then reduce to low heat, cover and simmer for approximately 20 minutes.

4. Add balsamic vinegar, sugar and basil.

Cannelloni

12 tubes	dried cannelloni
	Italian hard cheese to taste

Preheat oven to 180°C/350°F/Gas 4

1. Lightly cover with tomato sauce the bottom of a large baking dish.

2. Fill each cannelloni tube, using a teaspoon, with the spinach mixture.

3. Once all the tubes have been filled and arranged in the baking dish, evenly pour on the remainder of the tomato sauce. Grate some extra cheese on top and bake for 20–25 minutes or until the cheese is lightly browned.

Soya Butter Masala

Serves 6

140g (5 oz)	soya chunks
500g (1 lb 2 oz)	yoghurt
½	lime
1½ tsp	turmeric powder
½ tsp	cinnamon powder
½ tsp	ground paprika
½ tsp	black pepper
5 tbs	butter
1 tsp	oil
2 tbs	coriander seeds
2	bay leaves
4	cloves
6 pods	cardamom
2 sticks	cinnamon
2	green chillies
1	onion
2 tsp	ginger paste
3 cloves	garlic
1 tsp	coriander powder
1 tsp	red chilli powder
1 can (400g/14 oz)	canned chopped tomatoes
100ml (3½ fl oz)	fresh cream
	salt and pepper to taste

Method

1. Rinse soya chunks under cold water in a sieve. Put the soya chunks in a small saucepan full of boiling water, then reduce to medium heat and cook for 3–5 minutes or until they double in size and become soft and spongy. Drain and set aside.

2. Place yoghurt in a bowl and squeeze in the juice of ½ a lime. Add turmeric, cinnamon, paprika and black pepper, and mix well.

3. Squeeze the soya chunks to get rid of the excess liquid. Fold soya chunks into the yoghurt mix, cover and leave to marinate for at least an hour, or leave overnight.

4. Place the oil and 3 tbs of butter in a saucepan over medium heat. Crush coriander seeds and add to saucepan. Add the bay leaves, cloves, cardamom and

cinnamon sticks. Sauté the spices for a few minutes or until the aroma emerges and they turn light brown. Set aside.

5. Cut up the green chillies, onions and crush the garlic. Add these to the spices saucepan and cook on a medium to high heat for 30 seconds. Add the garlic and ginger paste to the saucepan and fry for another minute, stirring constantly to avoid sticking.

6. Add the coriander powder, red chilli powder and tomatoes to the saucepan and cook for 2–3 minutes or until the oil separates to the top, on high heat.

7. Allow the mixture to cool, then remove it from saucepan. Blend into a smooth purée.

8. Melt the remaining 2 tbs of butter in a large saucepan over a medium heat. Add the puréed mixture to the large saucepan and cook for two minutes. Add the marinated soya chunks, and set the remaining yoghurt marinade aside. Fry in the mixture for a few minutes or until the soya chunks start to colour a little.

9. Add the remaining yoghurt marinade and cook for 5 minutes on a low heat. Remove from the heat and mix in the fresh cream.

➤ *Serve hot with naan bread or rice.*

Paneer Butter Masala

    500g (1 lb 2 oz)   paneer
At step 1, replace soya chunks for paneer and slice paneer into medium sized chunks.
At step 3, marinate as above, then fry marinated paneer in a frying pan until browned on a medium to high heat.

Goat's Cheese, Tomato & Spinach Tarts
Serves 4

220g (8 oz)	spinach
280g (10 oz)	puff pastry
400g (14 oz)	passata
4 tsp	olive tapenade
110g (4 oz)	goat's cheese
	black pepper to taste

Preheat oven to 180°C/350°F/Gas 4

Method

1. Tear off spinach leaf from stalk and discard the stalks; blanch in boiling water for 30 seconds. Remove from the boiling water and rinse in a sieve with cold water immediately.

2. Roll out pastry until it is very thin and even. Cut into four rounds approximately 18–20 cm (7–8 inch) in size. Prick the surface of each round. Transfer each round onto baking tray a lined with parchment.

3. Spread each round with 3 tbs of passata and 1 tsp of tapenade evenly.

4. Squeeze the water out of the spinach, and divide it evenly onto the rounds. Slice the goat's cheese into thin slices. Overlap the slices on top of each round and cook for 10–15 minutes or until the cheese and pasty are slightly browned.

➤ *Serve hot with a drizzle of extra virgin olive oil, a few olives and basil leaves.*

Caramelised Onion & Goat's Cheese Tarts

250g (9 oz)	red onion
1 tbs	olive oil
¼ tsp	salt
1 tsp	sugar

At step 1, replace the spinach and olive tapenade with thinly sliced red onion. Heat oil in a frying pan. Add onions and sauté for 10 minutes over a low to medium heat, stirring occasionally to prevent burning. Add salt and sugar. Mix well and cook the onions for another 10 minutes or until they brown and caramelise.

Drizzle with a little balsamic vinegar and olive oil before serving.

Sage & Onion Tart

Serves 6

2 sheets	puff pastry
1.4kg (3 lbs 2 oz)	onions
3 tsp	dried sage
220g (8 oz)	extra mature cheddar cheese
65ml (2½ fl oz)	milk
	salt and pepper to taste

Preheat oven to 220°C/425°F/Gas 7

Method

1. Grease a 30cm x 22½cm (12 x 9 inch) baking tray with oil or butter.

2. Roll out a sheet of puff pastry and place in the greased baking tray, lightly piercing the pastry with a fork.

3. To form the pie shell, blind bake the pastry by covering it with foil or greaseproof paper and placing either pastry weights or uncooked beans or uncooked rice on top of the greaseproof paper to prevent the pastry from rising as it is baked. Cook for 15–20 minutes.

4. Remove from oven and carefully lift out foil or paper and pastry weights, beans or rice. Set aside to cool for 3–5 minutes.

5. Peel and slice onions into rounds and grate cheddar cheese. Place ¾ of the onions, dried sage, salt and pepper on top of the pastry. Sprinkle the cheese on top of the onions. Add the remaining onions on top of the cheese.

6. Roll out and cut the other sheet of puff pastry into 1½ cm (½ inch) strips. Criss-cross the strips over the whole filling to form a lattice.

7. Glaze the top of the pastry with milk using a pastry brush.

8. Bake for 15 minutes or until golden brown and crispy.

➤ *Can be served hot or cold.*

Vegetable & Tofu Pie

Pastry

310g (11 oz)	plain flour
1 tsp	salt
220g (8 oz)	butter
2 tbs	cold water

Preheat oven to 220°C/425°F/Gas 7

1. Sift flour into a large bowl. Chop butter into cubes. Add butter and salt to the flour.

2. Rub the butter into the flour, using your fingertips until you have a mixture that resembles coarse breadcrumbs.

3. Add cold water to the mixture, a few drops at a time until the dough comes together.

4. Wrap the dough in cling film and chill in the fridge for 30 minutes.

5. Roll out ¾ of the pastry to ½cm thickness, wrap the rest in cling film and refrigerate.

6. Lay the rolled out pastry into a 9-inch pie dish and gently press it into place. Trim any overhanging pastry, brush edges with cold water and place in fridge until ready to use.

Filling

500g (1 lb 2 oz)	tofu
125ml (4½ fl oz)	milk
4 tbs	arrowroot or cornflour
½ tsp	ground nutmeg
1 clove	garlic
½ tsp	salt
½ tsp	honey
2 tbs	vegetable oil
1	onion
370g (13 oz)	mushrooms
1	courgette
110g (4 oz)	carrots

220g (8 oz)	spinach
110g (4 oz)	cheddar cheese
110g (4 oz)	Emmental cheese
	salt and pepper to taste
	tamari to taste
	ground paprika to taste
	milk for coating

1. Blend tofu, milk, cornflour, nutmeg, garlic, salt and honey in a blender until creamy.

2. Finely slice onion mushrooms, courgettes and carrots.

3. Heat oil in a frying pan. Add onions and sauté for 4 to 5 minutes or until lightly browned, over a medium heat.

4. Add mushrooms, courgettes, carrots, spinach, tamari, salt and pepper. Cook the vegetables over a medium to high heat for 5 minutes or until all the liquid has evaporated. Remove the vegetables from the heat.

5. Grate cheddar and Emmental cheese. Mix the cheeses and the blended tofu into the frying pan.

6. Spread the mixture evenly into the pastry-lined pie dish and sprinkle paprika over the mixture.

7. Roll out the remaining pastry to ½cm thickness. Place it on top of the filled pie dish. Press the edges together, trimming any excess pastry. Lightly coat the top of the pie with milk, using a pastry brush. Bake for 30–40 minutes or until the pastry is golden on top.

Cheese & Onion Pie

5–7	onions
125ml (4½ oz)	milk
220g (8 oz)	cheddar cheese
	milk for coating

1. Make pastry as above, then replace the vegetables, tofu and spices with the filling below.

2. Finely slice onions. Add the milk and onions to a saucepan and bring to a boil over a high heat (this takes the sharpness out of the onions). Remove the saucepan from the heat and drain and discard the milk. Set onions aside to cool.

3. Grate cheese.

4. Layer the cheese and onions alternately into the pastry lined pie dish. Finish with a layer of cheese.

5. Roll out the remaining pastry to ½cm thickness. Place it on top of the filled pie

dish. Press the edges together, trimming any excess pastry. Lightly coat the top of the pie with milk, using a pastry brush. Bake for 30–40 minutes or until the pastry is golden on top.

Leek & Mushroom Pie

4	leeks
450g (1 lb)	mushrooms
60g (2 oz)	margarine
300ml (10½ fl oz)	vegetable stock
40g (1 oz)	plain flour
300ml (10½ fl oz)	milk
1 tbs	wholegrain mustard
	salt and pepper to taste

1. Make pastry as above, then replace the vegetables, tofu and spices with the filling below.

2. Slice leeks to 1cm (½ inch) thickness. Cut mushroom into quarters.

3. Melt margarine in a large frying pan. Add leeks and 225ml (8 fl oz) of vegetable stock. Cover the frying pan and cook for 5 minutes. Then remove the mixture and transfer into the pie dish.

4. Place mushrooms and 2 tbs of vegetable stock into the frying pan, cover and cook for 5 minutes. Remove only the mushrooms and place in the pie dish.

5. Add the remaining stock, plain flour and milk to the pan. Bring to a boil, whisking constantly to a smooth consistency. Simmer for a further 3 minutes and add mustard and salt and pepper to taste.

6. Pour the sauce over the leeks and mushrooms in the pie dish.

7. Roll out the remaining pastry to ½cm thickness. Place it on top of the filled pie dish. Press the edges together, trimming any excess pastry. Lightly coat the top of the pie with milk, using a pastry brush. Bake for 30–40 minutes or until the pastry is golden on top.

Mushroom Risotto

right

Serves 4

110g (4 oz)	mushrooms
1	onion
110g (4 oz)	cheese
2 tbs	oil
60g (2 oz)	butter
170g (6 oz)	risotto rice (carnaroli or arborio)
575ml (1 pint)	vegetable stock
110g (4 oz)	fresh or frozen peas
	salt and pepper to taste

Method

1. Finely slice mushrooms and onion. Grate cheese.

2. Fry mushrooms in oil and set aside.

3. Melt butter in a saucepan and lightly fry onions until light brown.

4. Add risotto rice to the saucepan and cook for a few minutes over a medium to high heat.

5. Add ¼ of the vegetable stock and salt and pepper to the saucepan and reduce the heat to low. Cook the rice until all the stock has been absorbed, stirring regularly.

6. Add another ¼ of vegetable stock to the rice and continue to cook over a low heat, stirring regularly. Add the remaining vegetable stock once the rice is creamy, plump and tender.

7. Fold in fresh or frozen peas. Continue to cook the rice for 20 minutes or until the vegetable stock has been absorbed, over a low heat.

8. Take the rice off the heat. Fold grated cheese and mushrooms into the rice.

➤ *Serve with shavings of cheese on top.*

Tofu Kebabs

1 clove	garlic
2 tbs	olive oil
1 tbs	lemon juice
2 tbs	tomato purée
1 tsp	dried oregano
400g (14 oz)	firm tofu
16	mushrooms
2	courgettes
4	tomatoes
1	green pepper
	salt and pepper to taste

Method

1. Crush garlic into a medium sized bowl. Pour olive oil, lemon juice, tomato purée, oregano, salt and pepper to the bowl and mix together thoroughly with a fork into an even marinade.

2. Slice tofu into 2½cm (1 inch) cubes. Place it in the marinade and toss the tofu gently until it is completely coated, taking care to not break up the cubes. Cover and leave it to marinate for at least an hour, or leave overnight.

3. Slice mushrooms and courgettes into 1cm (½ inch) rounds, quarter tomatoes and slice pepper into 2½cm (1 inch) squares.

4. Slide tofu and vegetables onto long skewers, alternating the pieces for variety. Brush the tofu and vegetables with any remaining marinade. Grill the skewers for 10 minutes, turning regularly, until slightly brown and charred.

Portobello Mushrooms & Halloumi

Serves 4

4	portobello mushrooms
I block	halloumi cheese
Icm (½ inch)	ginger
I clove	garlic
2 tbs	olive oil

Method

1. Cut the stalks off the mushrooms. Slice halloumi into thick slices. Grate ginger and garlic.

2. Heat oil in a frying pan. Add ginger and garlic and fry for a minute or until softened.

3. Place a thick slice of halloumi on the underside of each mushroom. Gently fry the mushroom, halloumi-side up, in the ginger and garlic, until the base of the mushroom is soft and brown.

4. Place the mushroom under the grill, halloumi-side up, until the halloumi is bubbling and golden.

Shepherd's Lentil Pie

Serves 6

Filling

2	onions
4 cloves	garlic
4	carrots
1 head	celery
200g (7 oz)	chestnut mushrooms
60g (2 oz)	butter
2	bay leaves
1 tbs	dried thyme
500g (1 lb 2 oz)	dried or canned green lentils
1.7 litres (2 pints 19 fl oz)	vegetable stock
3 tbs	tomato purée

Topping

2kg (4 lb 7 oz)	potatoes
80g (3 oz)	butter
100ml (3½ fl oz)	milk
60g (2 oz)	cheddar cheese
	salt and pepper to taste

Preheat oven to 190°C/375°F/Gas 5

Method

1. Finely chop onions and garlic cloves, dice carrots and celery and set aside.

2. Finely slice mushrooms and set aside separately.

3. For the sauce: Heat butter in a large saucepan. Fry onions, garlic, carrots and celery for 15 minutes or until the vegetables are cooked over a low heat. Add mushrooms and cook for further 4 minutes over a medium to high heat. Stir in bay leaves and dried thyme.

4. Thoroughly wash dry lentils. Add vegetable stock and lentils to the saucepan and cook over a low heat for 40–50 minutes or until lentils are very soft. If using canned lentils, drain, wash and add to the saucepan with the stock and cook over low heat for 10 minutes, or until lentils are soft.

5. Remove from the heat and stir in tomato purée and add salt and pepper to taste.

6. For the topping: place potatoes into a large saucepan and cover with water. Boil until the potatoes are cooked and tender. Drain and then peel and mash the potatoes in a bowl. Add butter, milk and salt and pepper. Mix thoroughly.

7. Pour the lentil mixture into a casserole dish and spread the mashed potatoes on top. Grate cheese and sprinkle on top.

8. Bake in the oven for 30 minutes or until the cheese potato topping is golden.

Cornish Pasties

Serves 8

Pastry

310g (10 oz)	plain flour
1 tsp	salt
220g (8 oz)	butter
2 tbs	cold water

Preheat oven to 220°C/425°F/Gas 7

1. Sift flour into a large bowl. Chop butter into cubes. Add the butter and salt to the flour.
2. Rub the butter into the flour, using your fingertips until you have a mixture that resembles coarse breadcrumbs.
3. Add cold water to the mixture, a few drops at a time until a dough forms.
4. Wrap the dough in cling film and chill in the fridge for 30 minutes.

Filling

1kg (2 lbs 4 oz)	potatoes
1	swede or turnip
4	onions
2	leeks
2 tbs	butter
220g (8 oz)	strong cheese
	salt and pepper to taste

1. Peel and dice potatoes, swede and onions into small pieces. Finely slice leeks.
2. Sauté leeks in butter until tender over medium heat. Set aside to cool.
3. Place all the vegetables in a bowl and mix well by hand.
4. Divide pastry into 8 balls. Roll out each ball to approximately 18cm (7 inch) rounds.
5. Place a small handful of vegetables into the centre of each round. Sprinkle 1 tbs of cheese, and salt and pepper to taste.
6. Dampen the edges of the pastry rounds with water and stick together by pinching the edges together.
7. Place on a parchment lined baking tray and bake for 45 minutes, then turn the heat down to 100°C/200°F and bake for a further 15 minutes.

Spinach & Cheese Pasties

1	onion
2 tbs	oil
480g (1 lb 1 oz)	spinach
340g (12 oz)	mozzarella cheese
480g (1 lb 1 oz)	ricotta

1. Make pastry as above and then replace the potato filling with the filling below.

2. Dice onion and grate mozzarella.

3. Heat the oil in a frying pan. Add onions and sauté over a low heat for a few minutes or until light brown.

4. Add spinach and cook for a further 1 minute or until wilted.

5. Drain the water from the spinach and onion and place in a bowl.

6. Add mozzarella and ricotta to the bowl and mix well.

7. Proceed from step 5 of Cornish Pasty.

Mushroom Pasties

2	onions
450g (1 lb)	mushrooms
80g (3 oz)	butter
60g (2 oz)	soya mince
1 tsp	dried mixed herbs
1 tbs	corn flour
120ml (4 fl oz)	milk
1 tbs	tomato purée
	salt and pepper to taste

1. Make pastry as above and then replace the potato filling with the filling below.

2. Dice onions, and slice mushrooms.

3. Heat oil in a frying pan. Add onions and sauté over a low heat for a few minutes or until light brown.

4. Add mushrooms, soya mince and mixed herbs to the frying pan, cover and cook for 5 minutes over a low to medium heat.

5. Mix corn flour and milk into a thick sauce. Add to the frying pan and mix until the mixture thickens.

6. Add tomato purée, salt and pepper to taste. Mix well, take off the heat and cool.

7. Proceed from step 5 of Cornish Pasty.

Macaroni Cheese

Serves 4

220g (8 oz)	macaroni
1 tbs	olive oil
80g (3 oz)	butter
170g (6 oz)	plain flour
2 tsp	dry mustard
500ml (17½ fl oz)	milk
450g (1 lb)	cheese
	salt and pepper to taste

Method

1. Add macaroni to a saucepan full of boiling water. Add oil and cook until al dente.

2. Drain macaroni but keep 225ml (8 fl oz) of the liquid from the cooked macaroni and set aside in a bowl.

3. Melt butter in a large saucepan. Add flour and mustard, and cook for a few minutes over a low heat, stirring constantly. Add milk and the liquid from the macaroni and cook until the mixture starts to thicken. Set aside.

4. Grate cheese. Stir 400g of cheese into the macaroni, in small quantities.

5. Stir in the flour, butter and milk mixture, and add salt and pepper to taste. If the mixture becomes too thick, add a little more water.

6. Place the macaroni in a flat ovenproof dish. Sprinkle with the remaining cheese and cook under the grill until brown.

Sweet & Sour Tofu

Sweet & Sour Sauce

2 tbs	cornflour
50ml (2 fl oz)	pineapple juice
2 tsp	soy sauce
50ml (2 fl oz)	water
3 tbs	ketchup
2 tbs	vinegar
1 tbs	sugar
1 tsp	olive oil

1. Combine all the ingredients in a saucepan and slowly bring to a boil, then lower the heat and simmer gently for 5 minutes or until sauce has thickened. Set aside.

Tofu

450g (1 lb)	tofu
110g (4 oz)	flour
1 tbs	cornflour
175ml (6 fl oz)	water
1 tbs	oil
	oil for frying

1. Cut tofu into 2cm (1 inch) cubes and set aside.

2. Mix flour, cornflour, water and oil in a bowl to make a smooth batter.

3. Toss the tofu in the flour batter until fully coated.

4. Deep fry battered tofu in hot oil until golden brown. Set aside to cool slightly.

5. Mix the tofu into the sweet and sour sauce.

➤ *Serve with rice.*

Paneer Tikka

Serves 4–6

Paneer

1½ tbs	butter
½ tsp	cardamom seeds
110g (4oz)	gram flour
125ml (4½ fl oz)	yoghurt
1 tsp	red chilli powder
2 tsp	ginger and garlic paste
1 tsp	tandoori masala
2 tsp	lemon juice
2 tbs	mustard oil
¼ tsp	turmeric powder
500g (1 lb 2oz)	paneer
	salt to taste
	oil for frying

1. Melt butter in a frying pan. Add cardamom seeds and gram flour and roast for a minute over a low heat, stirring continuously. Then remove from heat and set aside to cool.

2. Pour yoghurt, red chilli powder, ginger and garlic paste, tandoori masala, and lemon juice in a large bowl. Mix in the cardamom and gram flour mixture a tablespoon at a time. Add salt to taste.

3. Warm mustard oil in a heavy bottomed saucepan until it begins to smoke, then remove from heat.

4. Stir turmeric powder into the warm mustard oil. Mix this into the large marinade bowl.

5. Cut paneer into 2cm (1 inch) cubes. Mix the cubes into the marinade bowl, cover with cling film and place in the fridge for 1 to 2 hours.

6. Heat oil for frying on a flat iron pan (tawa), or frying pan. Place the paneer in the oil and cook over a medium heat until all sides are evenly browned. Set aside.

Sauce

4	onions
3	tomatoes
6 cloves	garlic
1 tbs	coriander leaves

2 tsp	vegetable oil
I tsp	cumin seeds
I ½ tsp	ginger and garlic paste
2 tbs	tomato purée
I tsp	red chilli powder
¼ tsp	turmeric powder
I tsp	coriander powder
I tsp	ground cumin
120ml (4 fl oz)	water
I tsp	dried fenugreek
I tsp	garam masala
90ml (3 fl oz)	cream
	salt to taste

1. Roughly chop onions and tomatoes, and finely chop garlic and coriander leaves. Crush fenugreek seeds.

2. Blend onions in a food processor.

3. Heat oil in a saucepan over a medium heat. Add cumin seeds and heat until browned. Add onions and sauté until well browned over a medium heat. Then add garlic and again cook until lightly browned. Add ginger and garlic paste and continue to sauté for another minute.

4. Mix in tomatoes and salt, and allow the sauce to start bubbling, then reduce to a low heat. Cover the saucepan and simmer until the tomatoes are soft and pulpy.

5. Add tomato purée, red chilli powder, turmeric powder, coriander powder, cumin powder and 60ml (2 fl oz) of water.

6. Cover the saucepan and cook for a few minutes or until the oil separates over a medium heat.

7. Mix in coriander leaves, fenugreek, garam masala, cream and the remaining water. Cook the sauce uncovered until it reaches the desired consistency, then take off the heat.

8. Gently combine the cooked paneer into the sauce.

➥ Serve with naan, chapati, or any other Indian bread.

Cheese & Parsnip Flan

Serves 8

280g (10 oz)	shortcrust pastry
3	large parsnips
110g (4 oz)	butter
170g (6 oz)	silken tofu
2	onions
2 cloves	garlic
pinch	dried or fresh sage
110g (4 oz)	strong cheddar cheese
	salt and pepper to taste
	flour for dusting

Preheat oven to 200°C/400°F/Gas 6

Method

1. Lightly dust a work surface with flour. Roll out the shortcrust pastry to ½cm thickness.

2. Press the pastry into a flan ring, pushing gently into the edges and sides of the tin. Prick the pastry with a fork and bake for 10 minutes until edges are lightly browned.

3. Peel and dice parsnips. Place in a saucepan and boil until soft. Drain and place in a large bowl.

4. Mash parsnips until fairly smooth. Mix in ½ the butter.

5. Mash silken tofu in a separate bowl until smooth. Set aside 1 tbs and mix the remainder into the parsnips.

6. Dice onions and crush garlic.

7. Melt remaining butter in a frying pan. Add onions, garlic, sage, salt and pepper and sauté until brown over a low heat. Remove from heat and add 1 tbs of tofu.

8. Place the mashed parsnip and tofu into a cooked flan ring. Cover with sautéed onions mix.

9. Grate cheese and sprinkle on top of the flan. Cook for 10 minutes at 180°C/350°F/Gas 4, or until the cheese is bubbling.

Sunflower Seed & Parsnip Flan
At step 10, replace the strong cheddar cheese for equal parts of sunflower seeds.

Deep Fried Tofu

Serves 3

280g (10 oz)	firm tofu
2 slices	bread
80g (3 oz)	gram flour
2 tsp	cumin seeds
1 tsp	coriander powder
1 tsp	turmeric powder
½ tsp	salt
½ tsp	garam masala
4 tbs	water
	sunflower oil for deep frying

Method

1. Slice tofu into long strips 2½cm (1 inch) thick.

2. Blend the bread in a food processor until it resembles fine breadcrumbs.

3. Mix gram flour, cumin seeds, coriander powder, turmeric powder, garam masala and salt in a bowl. Slowly add water to the bowl until you have a stiff batter.

4. Cover the tofu with the batter, then toss the battered tofu with in the breadcrumbs.

5. Heat oil in a saucepan over a high heat. To check if the oil is ready, put a tiny drop of batter into the saucepan, it should rise to the surface once the oil is hot enough.

6. Place the tofu pieces into a chip basket and lower into the oil. Fry for about 2 minutes or until the batter is golden brown.

7. Remove tofu from oil and place on kitchen paper to drain.

Lentil Burgers

Serves 4–6

200g (7 oz)	brown lentils
2	onions
80g (3 oz)	carrots
small handful	fresh parsley
2	potatoes
60g (2 oz)	breadcrumbs
	oil for frying
	salt and pepper to taste

Preheat oven to 190°C/375°F/Gas 5

Method

1. Wash brown lentils and place in a pan of water over high to medium heat. Bring to a boil and cook for 10 minutes then simmer for 20 minutes or until soft, over a low heat. Drain lentils in a sieve and set aside in a bowl.

2. Finely dice onions, grate carrots and chop parsley.

3. Heat a little oil in a frying pan. Sauté onions in oil until soft, over a low to medium heat.

4. Add grated carrots to the onions and fry for a further 2 to 3 minutes, then set aside.

5. Peel and chop potatoes. Add to a pan of boiling water and cook over a high heat for 10 to 12 minutes or until soft.

6. Drain and mash potatoes. Add parsley, salt and pepper. Mix in onions and carrots.

7. Gently crush lentils with a fork until they are coarsely mashed.

8. Mix lentils into the potato, onion and carrot mix.

9. Divide the mixture into 4 to 6 balls, depending on preferred size of burgers. Gently flatten each ball to form a patty.

10. Coat the patties in breadcrumbs. Place on a greased baking tray and bake for 20 minutes. Burgers can be shallow fried over a medium heat in a little oil until lightly browned.

➤ *Serve in a bun with salad and choice of condiments.*

Yeast Free Pizza Base

400g (14 oz)	plain flour
2 tsp	baking powder
1 tsp	salt
50ml (2 fl oz)	oil
185ml (6½ fl oz)	milk

Preheat oven to 220°C/425°F/Gas 7

Method

1. Mix together flour, baking powder and salt in a bowl.

2. Stir in oil and milk until the mixture leaves the sides of the bowl and starts to come together to form a ball.

3. Turn the dough onto a lightly floured surface and knead for 10 minutes or until it forms a smooth dough.

4. Divide dough into two balls. Roll each ball into a 30cm (13 inch) circle.

5. Place each base onto a baking sheet. Create the crust by turning up the edge by 1½cm (½ inch) and pinching.

6. Brush circles with 1 tbs oil. Apply the desired toppings and bake for 20 to 25 minutes or until base and toppings are browned.

Spinach & Mushroom Lasagne

Serves 2–3

8 sheets	lasagne
250g (9 oz)	spinach
1 tbs	salt
1 tsp	butter
1 tsp	dried marjoram
340g (12 oz)	ricotta cheese
	salt and pepper to taste

Sauce

170g (6 oz)	mushrooms
30g (1 oz)	butter
150ml (5½ fl oz)	vegetable stock
1 tsp	soy sauce
80g (3 oz)	cheddar cheese
	salt and pepper to taste

Preheat oven to 200°C/400°F/Gas 6

1. Cook lasagne for 8 to 10 minutes in a large pot of boiling water.

2. Drain lasagne sheets and rinse in cold water. Set aside.

3. Cook spinach in a dry frying pan for 6 to 8 minutes over medium-high heat.

4. Strain off excess water and chop finely. Return to frying pan and add salt.

5. Melt butter and marjoram in a separate frying pan stirring occasionally over a low heat. Once heated, remove from the heat and add ricotta and spinach.

6. For the sauce, melt butter in a saucepan and add sliced mushrooms. Cook over a medium heat for 10 minutes or until all the water has evaporated. Add vegetable stock and simmer for another 5 minutes.

7. Take off the heat and purée the mushrooms with a blender. Add soy sauce and salt and pepper to taste.

8. Lightly oil an oven-safe dish. Layer with the spinach filling, lasagne sheets and mushroom sauce. Repeat layering and finish with the mushroom sauce.

9. Grate cheese and sprinkle on top. Bake for 35 to 40 minutes.

➤ *Serve with salad or garlic bread.*

Cheese, Spinach & Mushroom Lasagne
At step 5, replace ricotta with a mixture of ½ cottage cheese and ½ cream cheese.

Spaghetti Bolognese

Serves 4

1	onion
3 cloves	garlic
½	red bell pepper
1	courgette
110g (4 oz)	mushrooms
2 tbs	olive oil
220g (8 oz)	soya mince
2	bay leaves
3 tsp	dried basil
2 tsp	dried oregano
2 cans (800g/1lb 12 oz)	canned chopped tomatoes
1 tbs	tomato purée
80g (3 oz)	spaghetti
	salt and pepper to taste

Method

1. Dice onion and crush garlic. Deseed and dice pepper, chop mushrooms and slice courgette in half lengthways then chop.

2. Heat oil in a saucepan. Add onion and garlic and cook for 5 minutes or until soft over a medium heat.

3. Add pepper, mushrooms and courgette to the saucepan and cook for 10 minutes or until the mushrooms are golden brown and all liquid has evaporated.

4. Add soya mince and herbs and cook for 4–5 minutes, stirring constantly. If the mixture sticks, add some of the juice from the chopped tomatoes.

5. Add chopped tomatoes and tomato purée. Stir well and simmer for 10 minutes over low heat.

6. Place spaghetti in a large pot of boiling water with a drizzle of olive oil and a pinch of salt. Cook for 10–12 minutes until al dente.

➤ *Garnish with cheese.*

Spaghetti & Tofu Balls

Serves 4

250g (9 oz)	firm tofu
I	onion
2 cloves	garlic
30g (I oz)	fresh parsley
I tsp	Dijon mustard
I tsp	ground cumin
I tbs	soy sauce
60g (2 oz)	ground almonds
2 tbs	olive oil
340g (12 oz)	spaghetti
	sea and pepper to taste

Sauce

I tbs	olive oil
I	onion
2 cloves	garlic
I	aubergine
2	courgettes
I	red bell pepper
I tbs	agave nectar
I can (400g/14 oz)	canned chopped tomatoes
200ml (7 fl oz)	vegetable stock
	salt and pepper to taste

1. Drain tofu, grate onion, crush garlic, and finely chop parsley. Add to a bowl. Mix in Dijon mustard, ground cumin, soy sauce and ground almonds, and mix until smooth. Add salt and pepper to taste. Divide and roll the mixture into 20 walnut-sized balls.

2. Heat olive oil in a large frying pan over medium heat and add the tofu balls. Cook gently, turning occasionally, until evenly browned. Remove balls from the frying pan and set aside.

3. For sauce, dice onion and crush garlic. Add to a frying pan with olive oil and cook over medium heat for 5 minutes, or until softened.

4. Dice aubergine, courgette, pepper and add to frying pan. Add agave nectar and fry for 10 minutes or until vegetables have softened and slightly browned. Season with salt and pepper.

5. Stir in chopped tomatoes and vegetable stock. Cover and simmer for 20 minutes until sauce has thickened.

6. Place tofu balls on top of the sauce. Cover and heat for a further 2–3 minutes.

7. Place spaghetti in a large pot of boiling water with a drizzle of olive oil and a pinch of salt. Cook for 10–12 minutes until al dente.

➤ *Garnish with torn basil leaves.*

Bubble & Squeak

Serves 8

1 kg (2 lbs 4 oz)	potatoes
400g (14 oz)	Brussels sprouts
4 tbs	butter
110g (4 oz)	plain flour
¼ tsp	olive oil
	salt and pepper to taste

Method

1. Peel and chop potatoes into bite-sized pieces, Add to a large pot of boiling water and cook for 12–15 minutes or until tender.

2. Drain the potatoes and return to the pot with the heat off. Cover with a tea towel for 2 to 3 minutes to dry.

3. Chop the ends off the Brussels sprouts. Add to a separate pot of boiling water and cook for 4 minutes. Drain and place in a bowl of ice water, to stop them from cooking. Drain then pat dry and finely slice the sprouts.

4. Add butter to the potatoes and mash well.

5. Add the Brussels sprouts and salt and pepper to taste. Leave to cool, then divide the mixture into 8 patties.

6. Mix flour with ¼ tsp of salt and pepper in a shallow dish. Roll each patty in the seasoned flour until covered.

7. Heat a ¼ tsp of oil in a large skillet or frying pan over a medium heat. Fry patties for 2–3 minutes on each side until golden brown.

Stir-Fry Noodles with Tofu

Serves 2

1cm (½ inch)	ginger
½ bunch	spring onions
110g (4oz)	button mushrooms
2 tbs	olive oil
2 tbs	sesame oil
220g (8oz)	pak choi
125g (5oz)	rice noodles
small bunch	fresh coriander
1 tbs	soy sauce
340g (12oz)	firm silken tofu
3 tbs	cornflour

Method

1. Peel and grate ginger, slice spring onions and slice button mushrooms.

2. Heat olive and sesame oil in a large wok or frying pan. Add ginger, onions and mushrooms.

3. Break pak choi into single leaves and add to the frying pan. Cover and simmer for 1–2 minutes or until the pak choi begins to wilt and the mushrooms are softened, over a low heat.

4. Add noodles, coriander and soy sauce to taste. Fry for a further 5 minutes or until cooked, stirring constantly. Set aside.

5. Cut tofu into 2–3cm (1 inch) cubes. Pat dry with a kitchen towel and turn in cornflour until all sides are covered.

6. Heat oil in a large frying pan. Fry tofu for 3–4 minutes or until golden over high heat, then add to the noodles.

➤ *Garnish with chopped red chilli.*

Asparagus Quiche

200g (7 oz)	shortcrust pastry
2 cans (800g/ 1lb 12oz)	canned asparagus spears
75g (3 oz)	cheese
2 tbs	flour
3 tbs	milk
	salt and pepper to taste

Preheat oven to 200°C/400°F/Gas 6

Method

1. Line a 20cm (8 inch) loose-bottomed flan tin with shortcrust pastry, riding it up the sides.

2. Prick pastry all over including sides and bake for 15 minutes. Remove from the oven.

3. Drain asparagus spears and arrange in the flan dish.

4. Grate cheese and sprinkle on top of the asparagus.

5. Sieve flour evenly across the flan. Spoon milk over the flour. Add salt and pepper to taste.

6. Bake for 15–20 minutes or until cheese starts browning.

Creamy Farfalle with Courgettes & Lemon   *Serves 2–3*

340g (12 oz)	courgettes
3 tbs	olive oil
200g (7 oz)	farfalle
½	lemon
80g (3 oz)	ricotta cheese
	salt and pepper to taste

Method

1. Thinly slice courgettes. Heat olive oil in a frying pan. Add courgettes and fry over medium heat, turning occasionally. Set aside.

2. Put farfalle, a drizzle of olive oil and pinch of salt in a large saucepan of boiling water. Cook the farfalle over a high heat for 10–12 minutes or until al dente.

3. Once cooked, drain farfalle and return to saucepan, with the heat off. Stir in courgettes with a splash of olive oil.

4. Grate and juice the lemon and add to the farfalle. Grate ricotta cheese and mix into the farfalle. Add salt and pepper to taste.

Jerk Tofu

Serves 6

4cm (1 ½ inch)	ginger
2 cloves	garlic
1	onion
2	red chillies
2 tsp	ground allspice
2 tsp	dried thyme
2 tsp	ground cayenne pepper
2 tsp	ground ginger
2 tsp	ground nutmeg
2 tsp	ground cinnamon
2 tbs	dark muscovado sugar
50ml (2 fl oz)	lime juice
50ml (2 fl oz)	soy sauce
100ml (3½ fl oz)	cider vinegar
1kg (2 lbs 4oz)	firm tofu

Preheat oven to 180°C/350°F/Gas 4

Method

1. Peel garlic and ginger, chop onion and deseed chillies. Add to a food processor.

2. Add allspice, thyme, cayenne, ginger, nutmeg, cinnamon, sugar, lime juice, soy sauce and vinegar to the food processor and blend into a paste. Set aside in a bowl.

3. Cut tofu to desired size and cover with the spice paste. Set aside to marinate at room temperature for 2–4 hours or overnight in a fridge.

4. Preheat oven to 180°C/350°F/Gas 4

5. Bake the marinated tofu in an oven safe dish for 30–35 minutes or until browned.

➤ *Serve with rice and vegetables or in a sandwich.*

Nut Wellington

Serves 4

340g (12 oz)	puff pastry
1	onion
2 sticks	celery
2 cloves	garlic
1 tbs	sunflower oil
110g (4 oz)	walnuts
110g (4 oz)	cashew nuts
170g (6 oz)	chestnut purée
1 tsp	ground paprika
1 tsp	dried oregano
2 tbs	lemon juice
1 tbs	cornflour
2 tbs	water
60g (2 oz)	button mushrooms
	milk for glazing
	salt and pepper to taste

Preheat oven to 220°C/425°F/Gas 7

Method

1. Roll out the puff pastry on a lightly floured surface. Line a loaf tin with the pastry, leaving enough over hanging to cover the top. Place in the fridge.

2. Heat oil in a frying pan on low. Chop onion, celery and garlic and fry for 5 minutes or until onions and celery are soft. Then place in a bowl.

3. Add walnuts, cashews, chestnut purée, paprika, oregano, lemon juice, salt and pepper to the bowl and mix well.

4. Combine cornflour and water until smooth. Add to the bowl.

5. Place mushrooms at the bottom of the pastry lined loaf tin. Top with the nut mixture, pressing it down firmly.

6. Brush the edges of the pastry with milk. Seal and cover with overhanging pastry.

7. Turn out the filled pastry onto a baking tray, with the sealed edge underneath.

8. Make two horizontal 4cm (1½ inch) cuts in the pastry and brush with milk.

9. Cook for 30 minutes, reduce temperature to 180°C/350°F/Gas 4 and cook for a further 30 minutes.

➤ *Serve with stuffed peppers & tomatoes, roast potatoes and Brussels sprouts.*

Sides

Houmous

Serves 12–14

220g (8 oz)	dried chickpeas
1	lemon
60g (2 oz)	tahini
1 clove	garlic
85ml (3 fl oz)	olive oil
	salt and pepper to taste

Method

1. Soak dried chickpeas in salted water in a pot overnight.

2. Drain and rinse chickpeas and put in a pot full of fresh water.

3. Boil for 10 minutes over high heat. Then reduce to low heat, cover and simmer for 1 hour, or until the chickpeas are very tender.

4. Drain chickpeas and rinse under cold water.

5. Blend the chickpeas, lemon juice, tahini and garlic in a food processor to produce a smooth paste. While blending, slowly pour in olive oil.

6. Salt and pepper to taste. Add lemon juice if desired. Sprinkle Paprika for colour.

Quick Houmous
At step 1, replace dried chickpeas with 2 cans of chickpeas (800g/1 lb 12 oz) and skip to step 3.

White Bean Houmous
At step 1, replace chickpeas with canned cannellini beans (220g/8 oz), add ½ tsp of ground cumin, omit water and add 150ml (5½ fl oz) of olive oil. Add salt and pepper to taste.

Sun-Dried Tomato Houmous
At step 5, add 100g (4 oz) of sun-dried tomatoes in oil. If using dry, re-hydrate in warm water before adding.

Potato Wedges

600g (1 lb 5 oz)	baking potatoes
3 tbs	olive oil
	salt and pepper to taste

Preheat oven to 200°C/400°F/Gas 6

Method

1. Wash and cut potatoes into chunky wedges.

2. Cook the potatoes in a pot of salted boiling water for 8 minutes over a high heat. Drain in a colander and set aside to dry for 2 minutes.

3. Place potato wedges on roasting tray. Drizzle with olive oil. Salt and pepper to taste.

4. Toss tray to coat wedges with oil and spread potatoes out evenly into a single layer.

5. Bake in the oven for 30 minutes or until golden, crisp and cooked through, turning occasionally.

Stuffed Tomatoes & Peppers

Serves 8

185g (7 oz)	basmati rice
1	onion
2½	red peppers
2½	green peppers
1	courgette
3	mushrooms
1	carrot
½ tsp	dried mixed herbs
4 tbs	olive oil
4	large tomatoes
8 slices	goat's or cheddar cheese
	salt and pepper to taste

Preheat oven to 180°C/350°F/Gas 4

Method

1. Cook rice in a saucepan of boiling water for 10 minutes over a high to medium heat. Drain and set aside.

2. Prepare filling by heating oil in a pan.

3. Finely chop onions, finely slice ½ red and green peppers, courgettes and mushrooms and grate the carrots.

4. Sauté the onions in a frying pan with olive oil for 4-5 minutes or until the onions are translucent and softened.

5. Fry the onions, peppers, courgettes, mushrooms and carrots to the saucepan with the dried herbs until soft. Salt and pepper to taste.

6. Remove from heat and mix with the rice. Set aside.

7. Slice the tops off the remaining red and green peppers and remove the white pith and seeds. Set the tops aside.

8. Slice the tops off the tomatoes and remove the seeds, setting aside the tops.

9. Stuff the tomatoes and peppers with the filling and cover with a thick slice of cheddar or goat's cheese before placing the tops back on.

10. Place stuffed peppers on a large baking tray or oven-proof dish with a little oil and bake in oven for 20–30 minutes, or until lightly browned.

Pan Haggerty (Potato Casserole)

Gf

220g (8 oz)	onions
450g (1 lb)	potatoes PEAS ?
170g (6 oz)	cheddar cheese
60g (2 oz)	butter
	salt and pepper to taste

Preheat oven to 190°C/375°F/Gas 5

Method

1. Peel and thinly slice onions and potatoes. Grate cheese.

2. Gently melt butter in an ovenproof frying pan over a medium-low heat. Add onions and fry for 10–15 minutes or until soft and golden.

3. Remove onions from the frying pan. Layer ⅓ of the potatoes in the buttery frying pan, followed by ½ the cooked onions and ½ the cheese and add salt and pepper to taste. Repeat the process finishing off with a layer of potatoes dotted with extra butter and cheese.

4. Place the ovenproof frying pan in the oven and bake for 30–40 minutes or until the potatoes are tender and cooked all the way through and the top is golden.

Mashed Potatoes

680g (1 lb 8oz)	potatoes
½ tsp	salt
4 tbs	cream
2 tbs	butter
100ml (3½ fl oz)	milk
	salt and pepper to taste

Method

1. Peel potatoes and cut into quarters.

2. Place potatoes in a saucepan adding salt and covering with water, over a high heat. Bring to a boil.

3. Once boiled, cover the saucepan and simmer for 15–20 minutes or until potatoes are soft, over a low heat.

4. Drain the potatoes, and set aside in a bowl.

5. Melt butter and cream together in a frying pan over a low heat. Mix into the potatoes.

6. Mash the potatoes with a potato masher until smooth. Beat further using a strong spoon.

7. Add milk to achieve the desired consistency and add salt and pepper to taste.

Polenta Fingers

Serves 4

4 tbs	olive oil
1 clove	garlic
1	red chilli
1 tbs	dried rosemary
800ml (1 pint 8 fl oz)	water
140g (5 oz)	quick cook polenta
110g (4 oz)	strong cheddar or hard goat's cheese
	salt and pepper to taste

Tomato Sauce

2 cloves	garlic
2 cans (800g/1 lb 12 oz)	canned plum tomatoes
2 tbs	olive oil
1	bay leaf
	salt and pepper to taste

Method

1. For the polenta, heat 2 tbs of olive oil in a frying pan over a low heat.

2. Chop garlic and deseeded chilli. Gently sauté in the frying pan over a low heat for 1–2 minutes, ensuring garlic does not brown. Add rosemary and remove from heat.

3. Boil water in a large saucepan. Add quick cook polenta, stirring constantly. Once smooth, simmer for 4–5 minutes stirring often. Set aside.

4. Grate cheese. Mix the fried garlic, chilli and rosemary and cheese into the polenta. Add salt and pepper to taste. Mix well.

5. Spread the polenta onto a cool plate evenly, and cool completely.

6. For the tomato sauce, chop garlic and crush tomatoes.

7. Heat oil in a frying pan. Fry garlic until soft but not browned. Then add crushed tomatoes and their juice. Add bay leaf.

8. Bring the tomatoes to a boil then simmer for 20–30 minutes, stirring occasionally. Add salt and pepper to taste.

9. Heat 2 tbs of olive oil in a frying pan. Cut the cooled, formed polenta into slices or wedges and fry for 2–4 minutes until light golden brown all over.

➤ *Serve with hot tomato sauce.*

Butter Bean, Lemon & Sage Pâté

4	shallots
2 cloves	garlic
small handful	fresh sage
2 cans (800g/1 lb 12oz)	canned butter beans
1	lemon
70ml (2½ fl oz)	olive oil
	salt and pepper to taste

Method

1. Finely chop onion, garlic and sage. Drain butter beans reserving 120ml (4 fl oz) of their liquid. Zest and juice the lemon.

2. Heat oil in a frying pan. Add onions and fry until soft, over a medium to low heat.

3. Add garlic, sage and lemon zest and fry gently for 5 minutes or until the garlic is soft.

4. Add butter beans and reserved liquid to the frying pan. Bring to boil over a high heat, then cover and simmer gently for 5 minutes over a low heat. Place in a bowl.

5. Mash the mixture in the bowl to a smooth paste (a few lumps are okay). Mix in lemon juice and remaining oil. Leave to cool completely.

➤ *Serve with crudités and toasted ciabatta or pitta bread.*

Artichoke Dip

1 can (400g/14 oz)	canned artichoke hearts
1 tbs	olive oil
200g (7 oz)	cream cheese
3 cloves	garlic
110g (4 oz)	vegan mayonnaise
1 tsp	vegetable stock powder
280g (10 oz)	artichoke hearts in oil
	salt and pepper to taste

Method

1. Drain the water from the canned artichoke hearts and place into a blender. Add olive oil, cream cheese, garlic, vegan mayonnaise, salt, pepper and vegetable stock to the blender. Blend until smooth.

2. Drain oil from jarred artichoke hearts and chop into small chunks.

3. Mix the chunks into the smooth dip.

➤ *Serve with rustic bread, crackers or flat bread.*

Baked Artichoke Dip

110g (4 oz)	Italian hard cheese
110g (4 oz)	mozzarella cheese

Preheat oven to 180°C/350°F/Gas 4

1. At step 3, grate cheeses and mix into the dip.

2. Pour dip into ovenproof dish and bake for 30–40 minutes or until golden and bubbling at the edges.

Baked Root Vegetables & Sweet Ginger Glaze   *Serves 3*

140g (5 oz)	sweet potato
1	potato
1	carrot
1	parsnip
1	turnip
2 tbs	olive oil

Glaze

60g (2 oz)	butter
2 tbs	caster sugar
1 tbs	fresh ginger
50ml (2 fl oz)	water

Preheat oven to 200°C/400°F/Gas 6

Method

1. Brush a large baking tray with oil. Peel and cut sweet potato, potato, carrot, parsnip and turnip into sticks (5cm x 2cm/2 x 1 inch).

2. Place vegetables baking tray and brush with olive oil. Bake for 40 minutes, turning regularly.

3. For the glaze, finely grate ginger. Melt butter in a small frying pan. Add caster sugar and stir until the sugar has dissolved over low heat.

4. Mix ginger and water into the frying pan. Bring to a boil, then simmer for 5 minutes or until the mixture has reduced and thickened slightly, over a low heat.

5. Remove roasted vegetables from oven. Coat with ginger glaze and serve hot.

Honey & Mustard Baked Root Vegetables

200g (7 oz)	clear honey
1 tbs	wholegrain mustard
	salt and pepper to taste

1. At step 1, remove potatoes from the recipe.

2. Mix honey, mustard, salt and pepper in a small bowl.

3. Bake the cut oiled vegetables in the oven for 20 minutes then remove the vegetables from oven. Coat with the honey and mustard glaze. Return to oven and bake for a further 20 minutes, turning occasionally.

Roasted Garlic Mushrooms

450g (1 lb)	button mushrooms
3 cloves	garlic
2 tbs	olive oil
2 tsp	salt and pepper
3 tbs	unsalted butter
2 tsp	lemon juice
60g (2 oz)	fresh flat leaf parsley

Preheat the oven to 230°C/450°F/Gas 8

Method

1. Place mushrooms in a baking dish.
2. Crush garlic cloves, chop parsley and squeeze the juice from the lemon.
3. Sprinkle garlic, oil and salt and pepper over the mushrooms. Gently toss the dish.
4. Cut butter into pieces and dot over the mushrooms.
5. Roast the mushrooms for 15–20 minutes in the oven, stirring occasionally.
6. Remove from oven and cover with lemon juice and chopped flat leaf parsley.

➠ *Serve hot*

Roasted Cashew Nut Pâté

Gf

Serves 4

110g (4 oz)	cashew nuts or roasted cashew nuts
1 clove	garlic
220g (8 oz)	cream cheese
small handful	fresh parsley
small handful	fresh chives
4 tbs	single cream
	Tabasco or hot pepper sauce to taste
	salt and pepper to taste

Method

1. To toast cashew nuts, bake in an oven until brown at 200°C/400°F/Gas 6. Or heat a frying pan and toast nuts until brown, over a medium to high heat. Cashew nuts can also be purchased ready-roasted.

2. Grind half the nuts in a pestle and mortar and chop the rest. Crush or finely chop garlic. Chop parsley and chives.

3. Beat cream cheese, single cream and crushed garlic in a bowl until smooth. Stir in nuts, Tabasco or hot pepper sauce and freshly chopped herbs. Add salt and pepper to taste.

4. Place in refrigerator to chill.

➤ *Serve with toast or slices of raw vegetables (celery, carrot or beetroot).*

Oven Baked Chips

Serves 4

3

potatoes
sunflower oil for drizzling
sea salt to taste

Preheat oven 200°C/400°F/Gas 6

Method

1. Peal and wash potatoes. Slice into 1cm (½ inch) thick slices, then cut into 1cm (½ inch) thick sticks.

2. Blanch in a large pan of boiling water for 3 minutes, then drain well.

3. Place potatoes in a roasting pan and lightly drizzle with oil, ensuring all chips are coated evenly.

4. Sprinkle with sea salt and bake for 15–20 minutes, turning at least twice until golden brown and crisp.

➻ *Serve hot with vinegar.*

Sweet Potato Chips
At step 1, replace potato with sweet potato.

Garlic & Rosemary Chips

2 cloves garlic
1 tsp dried rosemary

At step 3, crush garlic. Sprinkle garlic and rosemary over the potatoes. Bake the potatoes as above.

Roast Potatoes

Serves 4

1 kg (2 lb 4 oz)	potatoes
100ml (3½ fl oz)	olive oil
2 tsp	fine semolina
	sea salt to taste

Put roasting tin in oven and preheat oven to 200°C/400°F/Gas 6

Method

1. Peel and wash and cut potatoes into 8 even sized pieces. Place potatoes into a large pan full of cold water. Add salt and bring to a boil.

2. Once boiling, simmer for 4 minutes, over a low heat.

3. Drain potatoes and place in a large bowl.

4. Pour oil over potatoes and gently toss to evenly coat. Add semolina and sea salt and gently toss until evenly and thinly coated.

5. Carefully remove the hot roasting tin from oven and lightly cover with oil.

6. Place the potatoes into the hot roasting tin and spread in a single layer, making sure they have plenty of room.

7. Place potatoes in preheated oven and roast for 30–40 minutes, turning occasionally until golden and crisp.

Garlic & Rosemary Roast Potatoes

4 cloves	garlic
small handful	fresh rosemary

At step 4, crush garlic and chop rosemary leaves, add garlic and rosemary to the potatoes then continue to follow the rest of the recipe.

Cauliflower Cheese

Serves 4

1	cauliflower
500ml (17½ fl oz)	milk
4 tbs	flour
60g (2 oz)	butter
110g (4 oz)	cheddar cheese

Preheat oven to 220°C/425°F/Gas 7

Method

1. Remove leaves from cauliflower and cut florets into medium sized pieces. Wash thoroughly and set aside.

2. Bring a large saucepan of water to a boil. Add cauliflower and cook for 5 minutes or until soft. Drain and place cauliflower into an ovenproof dish.

3. Grate cheese.

4. Melt butter in a saucepan. Whisk in milk and flour stirring continuously until the sauce has a smooth and thick texture.

5. Whisk in 75g (3 oz) of cheese into the sauce and stir for a further 2 minutes or until the cheese melts.

6. Pour the sauce over the cauliflower. Sprinkle remaining cheese on top.

7. Place cauliflower cheese in oven and bake for 20 minutes or until bubbling with a golden crisp covering.

Breads

Avocado & Goat's Cheese Crostinis

Serves 4

Crostini

I	baguette
I clove	garlic
	extra virgin olive oil as required

Topping

2	avocado
100g (4oz)	goat's cheese
small bunch	fresh basil
I	red onion
I tbs	lemon juice
2 tbs	extra virgin olive oil
	salt and pepper to taste

Preheat oven to 180°C/350°F/Gas 4

1. Slice baguette into 2cm (1 inch) thick pieces, brush both sides with extra virgin olive oil and set aside in a baking tray.

2. Peel and finely chop garlic. Sprinkle garlic evenly on top of the baguette slices.

3. Place the baking tray in a preheated oven and bake for 5 minutes or until crisp and golden. Remove and leave to cool.

4. Peel and de-stone avocadoes. Mash avocado and goat's cheese together in a bowl and set aside.

5. Chop basil and finely dice red onion. Combine with avocado and goat's cheese mixture. Add olive oil, lemon juice and salt and pepper. Mix ingredients thoroughly.

6. Spread mixture evenly on top of the baguette slices and serve.

Potato & Onion Bread

110g (4 oz)	potatoes
1	small onion
500g (1 lb 2 oz)	strong plain bread flour
60g (2 oz)	butter
1 tsp	sugar
½ tbs	fast action dried yeast
300ml (10½ fl oz)	water
2 tbs	parmesan cheese
small handful	fresh thyme
	oil for frying
	milk for brushing
	salt and pepper to taste

Preheat oven to 200°C/400°F/Gas 6

Method

1. Peel and chop potatoes into small pieces and place in a pot. Add water, bring to a boil and simmer until cooked. Drain excess water and set potatoes aside to cool.

2. Mash the cooked potatoes until they are smooth and set aside.

3. Peel and finely chop onion. Sauté in a frying pan with oil over medium heat for 4–5 minutes or until lightly brown and transparent. Set cooked onions aside.

4. Sift flour into a bowl and add the butter. Using your fingertips, rub butter into the flour until mixture resembles breadcrumbs. Mix in the mashed potato, sugar, cheese, thyme, onion, salt and pepper.

5. Mix yeast with warm water. Make a well in the centre of the flour mixture and gradually mix in the warm yeast water to form soft dough.

6. Place the dough onto a lightly floured surface, knead for 5 minutes until smooth and elastic.

7. To make 2 loaves, evenly portion the dough or alternatively keep as 1 large loaf.

8. Place the dough onto a lightly floured baking tray and cover, leaving dough to proof (rise) in a warm place for 30 minutes or until it has doubled in size.

9. Brush the loaf with milk and top with thin slices of onion and thyme leaves.

10. Place baking tray in pre-heated oven, bake for 35–40 minutes or until cooked. When cooked the loaf will feel hollow when patted with a finger. Remove from oven, cool on a cooling rack.

Naan

Serves 6

300ml (10½ fl oz)	warm water
2 tsp	sugar
3 tsp	instant dried yeast
1 tbs	olive oil
200g (7 oz)	strong white bread flour
250g (9 oz)	plain white flour
1 tsp	salt

Method

1. Pour warm water into a large bowl, followed by sugar, yeast and oil. Mix ingredients together.

2. In another large bowl, mix both the strong white bread flour and plain white flour, then sprinkle salt over the mixture.

3. Pour the water to the flour mixture. Using your hands, mix together until the dough is soft and non-sticky. Add more water or flour until required consistency is reached.

4. Place the dough onto a lightly floured surface and knead for 5 minutes until smooth and elastic.

5. Place dough in lightly greased bowl and cover with a damp cloth/tea towel or greased cling film. Set aside in cool dry place for an hour or until the dough has doubled in size. Once the dough has risen, it can be kept in the fridge for up to 2 days.

6. Remove dough from the bowl and knead for 2 minutes. Separate the dough into 12 even balls on a lightly floured surface. Using a rolling-pin, roll out the dough in an oval shape approximately 23cm (9 inches) in length.

7. Place a flat iron pan (tawa) or a large frying pan on a medium-high heat.

8. Place the dough onto the hot frying pan and cook for a few minutes on each side. The naan should have scattered brown spots and should puff up a little on the pan while cooking.

9. Remove from pan, rub with butter, margarine or olive oil and serve hot.

Cheese Naan

| 200g (7 oz) | cheddar cheese |

At step 6, grate the cheese and set aside. Roll out the dough to the size of a palm and add a small amount of cheese, as a stuffing. Bring all the sides together forming a small ball. Using a rolling pin, roll out the dough in an oval shape approximately 23cm (9 inches) in length.

Garlic & Herb Naan

| 2 cloves | garlic |
| handful | fresh parsley |

At step 3, Peel and finely chop garlic; chop the parsley and add to the dough, mixing well.

Onion Naan

| 1 tbs | onion seeds |

At step 3, add 1 tbs of onion seeds to the dough.

Stuffed Focaccia

Serves 6–8

Dough

450g (1 lb)	strong plain white flour
2 tsp	fast action dried yeast
300ml (10½ fl oz)	warmed water
3 tbs	extra virgin olive oil
	coarse sea salt for sprinkling

1. Sift the flour into a bowl and stir in the dried yeast.

2. Make a well in the centre of the mixture and gradually mix in warmed water and oil to form soft dough.

3. Place dough onto a lightly floured surface and knead for 10 minutes until smooth and elastic. Place dough into a lightly greased bowl, cover and leave to proof in a warm place for 1½–2 hours or until doubled in size.

Filling

220g (8 oz)	frozen leaf spinach
220g (8 oz)	mozzarella cheese
handful	fresh oregano, rosemary and thyme
	salt and pepper to taste

Preheat oven to 220°C/425°F/Gas 7

1. Thaw and drain frozen spinach in a large strainer. Squeeze the spinach to remove any excess moisture and place in a bowl.

2. Dice cheese into small pieces and add to spinach.

3. Finely chop fresh herbs, add to the spinach mixture and season to taste with salt and pepper.

4. Lightly oil a 25cm (10 inch) round cake tin.

5. Remove the dough from the bowl and divide into 2 pieces. Roll out half the dough into a round shape, a little larger than the tin. Place the dough into the tin, pressing firmly onto the base and a 1½cm up the side.

6. Spread the filling over the dough to within 1cm (½ inch) of the edge.

7. Roll the second portion of dough into a 25cm (10 inch) round. Dampen the edge with water and place over the filling. Press edges together well to seal the 2 dough portions.

8. Lightly thumb indentations on the surface of the dough, brush with a little olive oil, sprinkle generously with sea salt and spray with water.

9. Place the baking tray in a pre-heated oven and bake for 30–35 minutes or until the dough has risen and is firm to the touch. Remove from the oven and leave in the tin for 10 minutes, then transfer to a wire rack to cool.

Cheese Scones

310g (11 oz)	self-raising flour
1 tsp	baking powder
75g (3 oz)	butter
110g (4 oz)	cheddar cheese
150ml (5½ fl oz)	milk

Preheat oven to 200°C/400°F/Gas 6

Method

1. Sift flour and baking powder into a bowl.

2. Cut the butter into small cubes and add to the flour. Using your fingertips, rub butter into the flour until mixture resembles breadcrumbs.

3. Grate cheese and add to the bowl and combine well.

4. Pour in milk slowly, mixing with a spoon until the mixture forms a soft dough.

5. Turn the dough onto a lightly floured surface and knead until smooth and elastic.

6. Roll out the dough to 1cm (½ inch) thickness, regularly dusting with flour to prevent sticking to work surface or rolling pin.

7. Using a 6cm (2½ inch) round pastry cutter, cut out shapes and place onto a baking tray, leaving 2cm spacing between each scone, allowing room for the scones to rise during baking.

8. Bring together the unused dough, knead lightly and repeat steps 6 and 7 until you have used all of the dough.

9. Brush the top of the scones with milk. Place the baking tray in a pre-heated oven and bake for 10–12 minutes or until the scones have risen and are golden brown. Remove from oven and transfer to a cooling rack.

Cheese & Spring Onion Scones
At step 3, finely slice 2 spring onions add to the bowl along with the cheese.

Sun-Dried Tomato & Cheese Scones

2 tsp	ground paprika
110g (4 oz)	sun-dried tomatoes

At step 1, add paprika or cayenne pepper to flour.
At step 3, chop sun-dried tomatoes, add the mixture together with the cheese.

Crumpets

350ml (12½ fl oz)	whole milk
225g (8 oz)	strong white flour
125g (5 oz)	plain flour
½ tbs	fast action dried yeast
½ tsp	fine sea salt
1 tsp	caster sugar
1 tsp	bicarbonate of soda
150ml (5½ fl oz)	warm water
	butter for greasing

Method

1. Warm milk gently in saucepan until tepid.

2. Sift strong white flour and plain flour into a bowl and stir in yeast, salt and sugar until well combined.

3. Make a well in the centre of the mixture and stir in the warm milk. Using a wooden spoon, work flour into the liquid gradually. Beat well for 3–4 minutes to make a smooth batter.

4. Cover bowl with cling film and set aside in a warm place for an hour for proofing, or until the batter has doubled in size.

5. Mix bicarbonate of soda with warm water and pour into the bowl. Beat the batter mixture for 2 minutes. Set aside to rest in a warm place for a further 30 minutes. The mixture will have raised and will also be covered in tiny air bubbles.

6. Heat a flat griddle pan or a frying pan over medium-high heat.

7. Generously butter the insides of 4 crumpet rings or 9cm (3½ inch) chefs' rings and place them onto the griddle or into the frying pan. Warm the rings for 2 minutes.

8. Using a dessert spoon, pour 3 large spoonfuls of the crumpet batter into each ring. The batter should come around 1½cm (½ inch) up the sides of each ring. Cook for 9–12 minutes, or until lots of tiny bubbles have risen to the surface and burst. The top of the crumpet will look dry and set.

9. Carefully lift off the rings; the crumpets will ease back from the sides when ready.

10. Flip the crumpets over and cook for a further 2 minutes, or until golden-brown.

➻ *Serve hot with butter. The crumpets can also be cooled and toasted.*

Cornbread

Makes 12–16 squares

500ml (17½ fl oz)	milk
2 tsp	apple cider vinegar
360g (13 oz)	cornmeal (polenta)
120g (4 oz)	unbleached all-purpose flour
2 tsp	baking powder
½ tsp	salt
85ml (3 fl oz)	vegetable oil
2 tbs	maple syrup

Preheat oven to 180°C/350°F/Gas 4

Method

1. Line a 23cm x 33cm (9×13 inch) baking tin with parchment paper.

2. Add milk and apple cider vinegar into a bowl and whisk thoroughly and set aside.

3. Sift cornmeal and flour in another bowl and add baking powder and salt, then set aside.

4. Add oil and maple syrup to the milk mixture. Whisk the mixture for 2 minutes or until foamy and bubbly.

5. Pour the milk mixture into the bowl with the dry ingredients. Mix all the ingredients together, using a large wooden spoon or firm spatula.

6. Pour the batter into the prepared baking tin. Place the baking tin in a pre-heated oven and bake for 30–35 minutes. To test if the cornbread is cooked, insert a toothpick into the centre of the tin; when the cornbread is thoroughly cooked the toothpick will come out clean.

7. Remove baking tin from oven and cool. Slice the cornbread into 12–16 squares.

Irish Soda Bread

Serves 6

170g (6 oz)	self-raising wholemeal flour
170g (6 oz)	plain flour
½ tsp	salt
½ tsp	bicarbonate of soda
290ml (10½ fl oz)	buttermilk

Preheat oven to 200°C/400°F/Gas 6

Method

1. Sift self-raising wholemeal flour and plain flour into a bowl. Add salt and bicarbonate of soda and mix well.

2. Make a well in the centre of the flour and pour in buttermilk, mixing quickly with a large fork to form soft dough. Add more milk if the dough seems too stiff. The dough should not be too moist or sticky.

3. Place dough onto a lightly floured surface and knead for 5 minutes until smooth and elastic. Form the dough into a round loaf shape.

4. Place the dough onto a lightly floured baking tray, then dust with flour.

5. With a small sharp knife, mark the top of the loaf with a cross about 1½cm (½ inch) deep.

6. Place the baking tray in a pre-heated oven and bake for 30 minutes or until the loaf sounds hollow when tapped.

7. Remove from oven and cool to room temperature to allow bread to set.

Tomato & Basil Bruschetta

Serves 6

350g (12 oz)	cherry or baby plum tomatoes
small bunch	fresh basil
½	lemon
6 slices	sourdough or ciabatta bread
2 cloves	garlic
	salt and pepper to taste
	extra virgin olive oil for drizzling

Method

1. Chop tomatoes into quarters and place in a bowl.

2. Chop basil, and pour the juice of half a lemon into the bowl. Add the olive oil and season with salt and pepper to taste. Mix ingredients together.

3. Toast bread on a griddle pan until golden brown and slightly charred.

4. Peel and crush garlic. Spread crushed garlic lightly over the slices of toasted bread and drizzle with extra virgin olive oil.

5. Spoon the seasoned tomatoes evenly over the toasted bread and serve warm.

Broad Bean & Cheese Bruschetta

170g (6 oz)	podded broad beans
30g (1 oz)	butter
2 tbs	olive oil
60g (2 oz)	ricotta or crumbly smoked cheese

1. At step 1, remove tomatoes, basil and lemon. Place broad beans in a pan of salted boiling water and cook on medium heat for 3–5 minutes or until tender.

2. Drain and cool, then remove skins and set aside.

3. Melt butter with oil in a pan over low heat.

4. Peel and finely chop garlic, add to frying pan and warm gently for 1–2 minutes.

5. Add beans to the pan and mix together over low heat for another 3 minutes.

6. Place beans in a food processor and blend into a coarse purée, adding more butter if required.

7. Toast bread on a griddle pan until golden brown and slightly charred.

8. Layer the warm purée over the slices of toasted bread. Top with ricotta and drizzle with olive oil.

Hot Cross Buns

Makes 10 Buns

800g (1 lb 12 oz)	plain flour
1 tsp	salt
1 tsp	ground allspice or mixed spice
60g (2 oz)	butter
80g (3 oz)	currants, raisins or sultanas
250ml (9 fl oz)	milk
30g (1 oz)	yeast
110g (4 oz)	sugar

Preheat oven to 190°C/375°F/Gas 5

Method

1. Sift flour into a large bowl and add salt and spice. Rub butter into flour using fingertips until it forms an even consistency. Add dried fruit and mix well.

2. Warm milk in a saucepan over a low to medium heat, taking care to not let it boil.

3. Remove milk from heat. Cream sugar and yeast together in a bowl and add to the warm milk. Leave to rest for 10 minutes, or until it has formed a sponge-like consistency.

4. Add the milk mixture to the flour mixture and work it with a spoon to form a dough. Cover with a tea towel and leave the dough to rise in a warm place for approximately 45–60 minutes, or until it has doubled in size,

5. Turn the dough out onto a floured surface and knead well, then cut into 10 pieces. Roll each piece into a ball between your palms then flatten into a circular bun shape. Using a knife, mark each piece deeply with a cross. Allow to stand on the floured surface for about 10 minutes.

6. Place the buns on a baking tray and bake for 15–20 minutes, taking care the buns do not burn on top.

➤ *Serve with butter.*

Condiments

Spiced Cranberry Sauce

1	chilli
½ stick	cinnamon
1	star anise
6	cloves
5cm (2 inch)	ginger
450g (1 lb)	sugar
225ml (8 fl oz)	water
100ml (3½ fl oz)	wine vinegar
450g (1 lb)	cranberries
	lemon juice to taste

Method

1. Place cinnamon, star anise, cloves, ginger and sliced chilli in a muslin bag.

2. Mix sugar, water and vinegar in a saucepan.

3. Place the bag of spices in the saucepan and bring to a boil over a high heat.

4. Add cranberries and cook until cranberries are soft over a low heat.

5. Add lemon juice to taste.

➤ *Serve chilled with nut Wellington or roast potatoes.*

Branston Pickle

250g (9 oz)	carrots
140g (5 oz)	turnips or swede
6 cloves	garlic
250g (9 oz)	cauliflower
250g (9 oz)	onion
200g (7 oz)	courgette
60g (2 oz)	dried apricots
60g (2 oz)	dates
80g (3 oz)	seedless raisins
200g (7 oz)	granny smith apple
60g (2 oz)	gherkins
220g (8 oz)	dark brown sugar
1 tsp	salt
50ml (2 fl oz)	lemon juice
650ml (1 pint 3 fl oz)	apple vinegar
60g (2 oz)	malt extract
2 tsp	black mustard seeds (or powder)
1 tbs	chili powder
1 tsp	ground cumin
2 tsp	ground allspice
1 tsp	ground black pepper
1 tbs	arrowroot powder

Method

1. Peel and chop all the fruit and vegetables into 3mm (⅛ inch) cubes.

2. Combine all the ingredients in a large saucepan and bring to a boil.

3. Cook the mixture over a low heat for 2 hours or until the swede and turnip are soft.

4. Stir well to redistribute all vegetables.

5. Bottle and seal in sterile jars.

➤ For an improved taste, allow pickle to age for a few weeks before eating. Serve with cheese, ploughman's lunches and in sandwiches.

Piccalilli

220g (8 oz)	cauliflower
280g (10 oz)	broccoli
2 bulbs	fennel
200g (7 oz)	fine green beans
140g (5 oz)	runner beans
310g (11 oz)	shallots
1	red onion
4	red chilies
2	green chilies
2 tbs	fine sea salt
2	apples
2	mangoes
3 cloves	garlic
2 tbs	mustard oil
2 tbs	mustard seeds
2 tbs	ground cumin
2 tbs	turmeric powder
½ tsp	ground nutmeg
2 tbs	English mustard powder
4 tbs	plain flour
500ml (17½ fl oz)	white wine vinegar
6 tbs	sugar
2 tbs	dried oregano
4	bay leaves

Method

1. Wash and break cauliflower and broccoli into small florets. Chop fennel, beans, shallots and onion into small chunks and slice chillies.

2. Put all vegetables in a bowl add salt and cover with water. Leave in a cool place for an hour.

3. Peel, stone and chop mango and grate apples. Peel and crush garlic. Set aside.

4. Heat mustard oil in a large saucepan. Fry mustard seeds, cumin, turmeric and nutmeg for a moment, then lower the heat.

5. Add mustard powder, flour and a splash of vinegar. Stir well to make a thick paste. Gradually add the remaining vinegar and 100ml of water, stirring constantly to produce a smooth paste.

6. Add apples, mangoes, sugar, garlic, oregano and bay leaves. Cook for 2–3 minutes.

7. Drain the salted vegetables and add to the saucepan, stirring well to evenly coat with the paste.

8. Cook for 10–15 minutes or until the vegetables have softened and started to release some juice.

9. Bottle and seal in sterile jars.

Pickled Onions

450g (1 lb)	shallots
60g (2 oz)	salt
500ml (17½ fl oz)	malt vinegar
200g (7 oz)	clear honey

Method

1. Place shallots in a large heatproof bowl and cover with boiling water. Set aside. Once cool, trim the roots and tops, and peel. Sprinkle salt over the peeled onions, stir and leave overnight.

2. Rinse onions well and dry. Pack onions into clean, sterilized jars.

3. Place vinegar and honey into a saucepan and gently heat; do not boil.

4. Pour the hot vinegar mixture into the onion jars and check there are no air pockets. Seal jars and leave to cool.

5. The onions will be ready to eat after approximately a month. Once opened, store in fridge.

Apple Sauce

220g (8 oz)	cooking apples
½	lemon
2 tbs	water
15g (½ oz)	butter
I tsp	caster sugar

Method

1. Peel, core and chop apples. Zest the lemon.

2. Place apples in a saucepan with lemon zest and water. Cover and cook over a low heat until apples are soft and mushy.

3. Take off the heat and beat in butter and sugar.

➤ *Serve cool.*

Pesto

10g	cashew or pine nuts
50ml (2 fl oz)	extra virgin olive oil
30g	fresh basil
2 cloves	garlic
½ tsp	salt
	black pepper to taste

Method

1. Gently toast cashew or pine nuts in a dry frying pan until golden over a medium heat.

2. Place basil, garlic, toasted nuts and a little oil in blender and blend into a smooth paste.

3. Add salt, black pepper and remaining oil to the blender.

4. Allow the paste to stand for a few hours.

House Vegan Mayonnaise

125ml (4½ fl oz)	soya milk
1 tsp	Dijon mustard
½ tsp	cider vinegar
200ml (7 fl oz)	vegetable oil
	salt to taste

Method

1. Mix soya milk, mustard and vinegar in a blender at high speed.

2. Slowly add oil, until the mixture is thick and creamy. Add extra oil if needed and add salt to taste.

➤ *The mayonnaise can be used immediately or placed in an airtight container and stored for 3–4 weeks in a fridge.*

Mint Chutney

1½ tsp	pomegranate seeds or mango powder
110g (4oz)	red onion
30g (1 oz)	fresh mint leaves
4	green chilies
2 tsp	sugar
¾ tsp	salt
75ml (3 fl oz)	water
30g (1 oz)	fresh coriander

Method

1. Grind pomegranate seeds and roughly chop onion. Add to a blender.

2. Add mint, chillies, sugar, salt water and coriander and blend until smooth and combined.

Yoghurt Mint Chutney
At step 2, add 1 tbs of chutney to 100g (4oz) of yoghurt and mix well.

Onion Gravy

2	onions
2 tbs	vegetable oil
2 tbs	butter
1 tsp	sugar
1 tsp	balsamic vinegar
750ml (1 pint 6 fl oz)	vegetable stock
4 tsp	corn flour
4 tsp	cold water
	salt and pepper to taste

Method

1. Peel and thinly slice onions.

2. Heat oil and butter in a large saucepan over a medium to low heat. Add onions, cover and cook for approximately 10 minutes or until the onions are soft and translucent, stirring occasionally, not letting the onions brown.

3. Add sugar and balsamic vinegar. Cover and cook for a further 5 minutes, stirring occasionally, ensuring the mixture does not burn.

4. Add stock and bring to a boil over a high heat. Then gently simmer for 5 minutes uncovered, over a low heat.

5. Mix corn flour with cold water to create a thin paste in a heatproof bowl. Mix a spoonful of the hot onion liquid into the flour mixture Pour the flour mixture into the onions and stir until smooth.

6. Bring the mixture to a boil over a high heat. Then gently simmer for 10 minutes until the mixture thickens, over a low heat.

7. Add salt and pepper to taste.

➤ *Keep warm until ready to serve. To create glossy gravy, whisk 1 tsp of chilled butter into gravy before serving.*

Mushroom Gravy

110g (4 oz)	mushrooms
4 tsp	olive oil
2 tbs	plain flour
225ml (8 fl oz)	vegetable stock
½ tsp	dried oregano
½ tsp	dried tarragon
	salt and pepper to taste

Method

1. Finely slice mushrooms.

2. Add 2 tsp of oil to a frying pan. Sauté mushrooms in the frying pan until their water has evaporated over a medium heat. Set aside.

3. Add the remaining 2 tsp of oil to a separate frying pan over a low heat. Add flour and stir constantly for 1 minute.

4. Slowly add vegetable stock, stirring constantly. Bring the mixture to a boil over a high heat and then remove from heat.

5. Add herbs, salt and pepper to taste. Stir in sautéed mushrooms.

Desserts

Almond Macaroons

60g (2 oz)	semolina
60g (2 oz)	ground almonds
80g (3 oz)	caster sugar
1 tsp	baking powder
½ tsp	almond essence
5 tbs	cold water
12	blanched almonds

Preheat oven to 165°C/325°F/Gas 3

Method

1. Cover baking tray with rice paper.

2. Mix semolina, ground almonds, caster sugar and baking powder in a bowl.

3. Add almond essence and water to the ingredients and combine to a soft consistency.

4. Put 1 tsp of the mixture onto the rice paper, roughly shaping it into a circle. Leave some room for the macaroons to spread out during baking.

5. Place the baking tray in a pre-heated oven and bake for 12 minutes or until golden brown on top. Remove from the oven. Place an almond on top of each biscuit.

Ginger Snaps

Makes 12

60g (2 oz)	butter
60g (2 oz)	sugar
60g (2 oz)	golden syrup
60g (2 oz)	flour
1 tsp	ground ginger

Preheat oven to 150°C/300°F/Gas 2

Method

1. Melt butter in a saucepan over low heat.

2. Add sugar and syrup to the saucepan. Mix ingredients to form a smooth consistency. Remove from heat.

3. Add flour and ginger, combine ingredients.

4. Place 1 tsp of mixture onto a greased baking sheet, at a time and 5cm (2 inches) apart allowing the mixture to spread.

5. Place the baking tray in a preheated oven and bake for 12 minutes or until brown.

6. Whilst the snaps are still warm, roll them round a wooden spoon handle to form hollow tubes. Fill the tubes with whipped cream.

Cranberry Flapjacks

280g (10 oz)	butter
170g (6 oz)	soft dark brown sugar
80g (3 oz)	treacle or black strap molasses
80g (3 oz)	golden syrup
60g (2 oz)	dried cranberries
450g (1 lb)	porridge oats
4 tbs	flour
60g (2 oz)	desiccated coconut

Preheat oven to 190°C/375°F/Gas 5

Method

1. Melt butter in a saucepan, on low heat. Add sugar, treacle, syrup and cranberries, stirring continuously.

2. Add porridge oats, flour and coconut. Mix ingredients thoroughly.

3. Pour the mixture into a baking tray, spreading evenly using the back of a spoon.

4. Place the baking tray in a preheated oven and bake for 25–30 minutes.

5. Remove from oven and cool a little before cutting into rectangles. Place on a wire tray to cool completely.

Flapjacks

110g (4 oz)	butter
110g (4 oz)	demerara sugar
5 tbs	golden syrup
220g (8 oz)	porridge oats

Preheat oven to 190°C/375°F/Gas 5

Method

1. Grease a 20cm (8 inch) baking tray.

2. Melt butter in a large pan over low heat. Add sugar and syrup, stir until ingredients have dissolved

3. Add porridge oats and mix well.

4. Pour the mixture into the baking tray; spread evenly using the back of a spoon.

5. Place the baking tray in a preheated oven and bake for 20 minutes.

6. Remove from the oven and allow to cool for 15 minutes. Cut into 8 wedge pieces.

7. When the flapjacks are completely cool, turn them out of the tin and break into wedges.

Chocolate Flapjacks

At step 6, Melt 200g of dark chocolate in a heatproof bowl over a saucepan of boiling water. Pour over the flapjacks once baked and slightly cooled, before cutting into wedges. Place in the fridge to cool completely and set. Cut into 8 wedge pieces.

Ginger Flapjacks

ground ginger	1 tsp
crystallised ginger	60g (2 oz)

At step 3, Finely chop crystallised ginger. Add ginger and ground ginger with the oats.

Fruit & Nut Biscuits

Makes 24

110g (4oz)	margarine
60g (2oz)	sugar
1 tbs	golden syrup
1 tbs	milk
1 tsp	bicarbonate of soda
220g (8oz)	self-raising flour
2 tbs	chopped nuts and raisins

Preheat oven to 180°C/350°F/Gas 4

Method

1. Add margarine, sugar, syrup and milk into a saucepan and heat, but do not boil.

2. Add bicarbonate of soda and mix until ingredients froth. Remove from heat.

3. Stir in flour, chopped nuts and raisins; continue stirring until the mixture does not stick to the side of the pan.

4. Place 1 tsp of mixture onto a greased baking tray, spaced well apart.

5. Place the baking tray in a preheated oven and bake for 15 minutes or until golden brown.

6. Remove from the oven and allow to cool on a wire rack.

Florentines

Gf

90g (3 oz)	butter
110g (4 oz)	caster sugar
90g (3 oz)	candied mixed peel
30g (1 oz)	glacé cherries
90g (3 oz)	chopped almonds
2 tbs	whipped cream
170g (6 oz)	plain dark chocolate

Preheat oven to 180°C/350°F/Gas 4

Method

1. Melt butter in a saucepan over low heat. Add sugar and stir until the sugar has dissolved. Remove from heat.

2. Chop the glacé cherries into quarters. Add cherries and almonds, combining the ingredients. Add in whipped cream and mix well.

3. Place 1 tsp of mixture on a greased baking tray, spaced well apart. Bake for 3–4 minutes.

4. Remove from oven. Tidy the Florentine biscuit edges with a fork pressing the mixture into the center. Bake for another 4 minutes, then cool on a wire tray.

5. Melt plain dark chocolate in a bowl over a saucepan of hot water. Spread chocolate smoothly over the cooled biscuits, making a wavy lined pattern using a fork.

6. Store in an airtight tin to keep the biscuits crisp.

Jammie Dodgers

Makes 4

125g (5 oz)	unsalted butter
60g (2 oz)	caster sugar
125g (5 oz)	plain or spelt flour
60g (2 oz)	fine semolina
6 tsp	strawberry jam

Preheat oven to 180°C/350°F/Gas 4

Method

1. Line a baking tray with parchment paper and set aside.

2. Beat the butter and sugar in a bowl until pale and fluffy.

3. Add the flour and semolina; beat until the dough comes together to form a ball.

4. Divide the dough into 2 evenly sized pieces. Squash into evenly sized flat discs. Place each disc between 2 pieces of baking parchment and chill in the fridge for 25 minutes.

5. Remove dough from the fridge, roll out the discs into 5cm (2 inch) circles thick.

6. Using a large heart shaped or round biscuit cutter, cut out 8 biscuits and place 4 on the baking tray.

7. With the remaining 4 biscuits, cut a 2cm (1 inch) heart or circle out of the centre of the dough. Sprinkle with caster sugar then place onto the baking tray.

8. Place the tray in the fridge or freezer for 15–20 minutes to firm up the dough.

9. Place the baking tray in a preheated oven and bake for 12–15 minutes or until pale gold. Remove from the oven and leave to cool on the baking tray.

10. Once cooled, spread 1½ tsp of strawberry jam onto each biscuit leaving a 1cm (½ inch) border around the edge. Sandwich the cut out biscuits on top (sugar side up) and press together.

11. The biscuits will remain fresh in an airtight container for up to 1 week.

Quick Shortbread

110g (4 oz)	butter
150g (5 oz)	plain or spelt flour
25g (1 oz)	cornflour
50g (2 oz)	caster sugar

Preheat oven to 190°C/375°F/Gas 5

Method

1. Melt butter in a bowl over a saucepan of hot water.

2. Remove the bowl and add the flour, cornflour and sugar. Mix the ingredients into a soft dough.

3. Press the dough into a 20cm (8 inch) baking tin. Prick the mixture with a fork and place the baking tin in a preheated oven and bake for 25 minutes or until the edges turn golden brown.

4. Remove from the oven and cool on a wire rack.

5. Sprinkle with caster sugar.

Treacle Spice Biscuits

200g (7 oz)	plain flour
½ tsp	baking powder
½ tsp	ground ginger
½ tsp	ground cinnamon
½ tsp	ground mixed spice
60g (2 oz)	muscovado sugar
110g (4 oz)	butter
60g (2 oz)	black treacle or molasses

Preheat oven to 165°C/325°F/Gas 3

Method

1. Sift the flour in a bowl. Add baking powder, all spices and sugar mixing ingredients well.

2. Add diced butter to the bowl. Using your fingertips, rub the ingredients together until the mixture resembles fine breadcrumbs.

3. Make a well in the centre and add the treacle or molasses. Using your hands, mix the dough well.

4. Turn the dough out onto a lightly floured surface and knead until there are no streaks of treacle in the dough.

5. Divide the dough into 2 evenly sized pieces and squash into evenly sized flat discs. Place each disc between 2 pieces of baking parchment and chill in the fridge for 25 minutes.

6. Once chilled, roll out each disc between the baking parchments.

7. Using a cookie cutter, cut out heart or star shapes. If you are going to hang the biscuits on a Christmas tree, make a clear hole near the top of each biscuit using a skewer.

8. Place the baking tray in a preheated oven and bake for 10–12 minutes.

9. Remove from the oven and allow the cookie o cool on a wire rack.

Cinnamon Sugar Apple Cake

Serves 8–10

Cake

110g (4 oz)	butter
150ml (5½ fl oz)	milk
2 tbs	apple cider vinegar
220g (8 oz)	self-raising flour
3 tsp	baking powder
2–3	bramley cooking apples
30g (1 oz)	sugar

Preheat the oven to 200°C/400°F/Gas 6

1. Grease and flour a 20cm x 30cm (8 x 12 inch) baking tin.

2. Bring butter and milk to boil in a saucepan and stir occasionally. Add the apple cider vinegar bringing the mixture to boil. Remove from heat and set aside.

3. Sieve flour and baking powder into the liquid mixture and fold until there are no lumps of flour. Pour the mixture into the baking tin.

4. Peel, core and cut apples into thin slices, arranging them so that they overlap on top of the batter. Sprinkle sugar on top.

5. Place the baking tray in a preheated oven and bake for 10 minutes. Reduce heat to 180°C/350°F/Gas 4 and bake for a further 20–25 minutes or until risen and golden brown.

Cinnamon Sugar

¼ tsp	ground cinnamon
30g (1 oz)	caster sugar

1. Combine cinnamon and sugar and sprinkle on top of the baked cake.

➤ *Serve warm with cream or custard.*

Apple Pie

Serves 4–6

Pastry

110g (4 oz)	margarine
220g (8 oz)	plain flour
6 tsp	water

1. Cut margarine into cubes, place all ingredients in freezer for 30 minutes before making pastry.

2. Remove all ingredients from the freezer. Add the margarine and flour into a bowl.

3. Using your fingers, mix the margarine into the flour until it resembles breadcrumbs.

4. Add 1 tsp of water at a time until the mixture forms a dough (you may not need all the water).

5. Wrap the dough in cling film and refrigerate whilst preparing the filling.

Filling

680g (1 lb 8 oz)	cooking apples
2 tbs	water
6	cloves (optional)
8 heads	elderflower (optional)
80g (3 oz)	sugar
	milk for glazing

Preheat oven to 200°C/400°F/Gas 6

1. Peel, core and slice apples. Place apples in a pan with water, cloves and elderflower (if using).

2. Heat and cook for 5 minutes or until the apples to soften. Remove the elderflower.

3. Place the softened apple in a baking pie dish in layers and sprinkle each layer with sugar.

4. Remove the pastry from the fridge and unwrap the cling film.

5. Turn the dough out onto a lightly floured surface and roll out the pastry slightly larger than size of the baking flan dish.

6. Brush the rim of the pie dish with water. Lift the pastry onto the rolling pin and place over apples, pressing gently round the rim. Roll up the overhanging pastry into a tidy crust.

7. Brush the top of the pie with milk and sprinkle with sugar. Cut 3 slits into top of the pastry.

8. Place the baking flan dish in a preheated oven and bake for 30–40 minutes or until golden brown on top.

Blackberry & Apple Pie

220g (8oz)	blackberries
450g (1 lb)	cooking apples

At step 3, add blackberries to the baking dish as the apple layers are set.

Plum, Rhubarb, Gooseberry & Blackcurrant Pie

220g (8oz)	plums
220g (8oz)	rhubarb
110g (4oz)	gooseberries
110g (4oz)	blackcurrants
190g (7oz)	sugar (extra)

At step 1, replace cooking apples, elderflower and cloves for plums, rhubarb and berries.
At step 3, add extra sugar.

Blackberry & Apple Crumble

Serves 6–8

600g (1 lb 5 oz)	bramley apples
250g (9 oz)	blackberries
30g (1 oz)	caster sugar
110g (4 oz)	plain flour
60g (2 oz)	brown sugar
60g (2 oz)	butter
60g (2 oz)	ground almonds
110g (4 oz)	porridge oats

Preheat oven to 180°C/350°F/Gas 4

Method

1. Peel, core and cut apples into 1cm (1/2 in) pieces into a bowl.

2. Add blackberries and caster sugar into the bowl and mix ingredients well. Transfer the fruit mix to a deep ovenproof dish.

3. Put the flour, brown sugar, butter and almonds into a food processor and pulse until the mixture resembles breadcrumbs.

4. Stir in porridge oats into the mixture. Combine well.

5. Sprinkle the crumble evenly over the fruit.

6. Place the ovenproof dish in a preheated oven and bake for 35–40 minutes or until the topping is crisp and golden brown.

▶ *Serve with ice cream or custard.*

Bakewell Tart

110g (4 oz)	margarine
220g (8 oz)	self-raising flour
2–4 tbs	water
6 tbs	plum or blackcurrant jam
110g (4 oz)	butter
110g (4 oz)	sugar
60g (2 oz)	ground rice
80g (3 oz)	ground almonds
60g (2 oz)	desiccated coconut
2 tbs	milk
2 tbs	single cream
¼ tsp	almond essence
80g (3 oz)	glacé cherries
80g (3 oz)	almond flakes

Preheat oven to 190°C/375°F/Gas 5

Method

1. Add margarine and self-raising flour into a bowl. Add 1 tbs of water at a time, mixing the ingredients to form soft dough.

2. Turn the dough out onto a lightly floured surface and roll out the pastry. Lift the pastry into a baking flan dish, cutting off any overhanging pastry.

3. Layer the bottom of the pie with jam, then place the dish in the fridge.

4. Cream the butter and sugar together in a bowl until light and fluffy.

5. Sieve ground rice and ground almonds into the butter mix and add desiccated coconut. Fold until ingredients are mixed well.

6. Pour in milk, cream and almond essence into the bowl and mix well

7. Add halved cherries and almond flakes to the bowl; combine well.

8. Spread the mixture into the pie dish, on top of the jam.

9. Place the baking flan dish in a preheated oven and bake for 30–35 minutes.

Luxury Treacle Tarts

Pastry

225g (8 oz)	plain or spelt flour
110g (4 oz)	butter
2 tbs	water
¼ tsp	salt

Preheat oven to 190°C/375°F/Gas 5

1. Grease a 25½cm (10 inch), or four 13cm (5 inch) loose bottomed flan tins and place on a baking tray.

2. Add flour and butter to a bowl. Using your fingers, mix the butter into the flour until it resembles fine breadcrumbs. Add water and salt and combine the mixture.

3. Turn the mixture out onto a lightly floured surface and knead for 5 minutes to form a smooth dough. Wrap in cling-film and place in the fridge for 30 minutes.

4. Once chilled, roll out the pastry to generously fit the tins. Gently ease the pastry into the tin, allowing some to fall over the sides.

5. Trim the pastry around the edges of each tin with a sharp knife, then prick the pastry bases with a fork.

6. Line the pastry cases with greaseproof paper and fill with pastry weights or dried pulses. Place the baking tray in a preheated oven and bake for 15 minutes. Remove the paper and weights and return to the oven for a further 5 minutes. Remove and leave to cool.

Filling

1	lemon
500g (1 lb 2 oz)	golden syrup
125g (5 oz)	breadcrumbs
25g (1 oz)	pecans
4 tsp	apple cider vinegar
3 tbs	double cream
¼ tsp	salt

1. Juice lemon and grate the zest into a large bowl. Add golden syrup, breadcrumbs, finely chopped pecans, cider vinegar, double cream and salt. Mix thoroughly.

2. Pour mixture into the pastry cases and bake for 20 minutes or until filling is lightly browned.

➤ *Serve with crème fraîche or custard.*

Cream Tea

Makes 8

220g (8 oz)	self-raising flour
¼ tsp	salt
60g (2 oz)	unsalted butter
50ml (2 fl oz)	whole milk
30g (1 oz)	caster sugar

Preheat oven to 220°C/425°F/Gas 7

Method

1. Sift the flour and salt into a large bowl.

2. Dice the fridge-temperature butter into cubes and add to the bowl. Using your fingers, mix the butter into the flour until it resembles breadcrumbs. Mix in sugar.

3. Make a well in the centre of the crumbs and pour in the milk. Quickly bring the mixture together to form a soft dough using a palette or table knife

4. Turn the dough out onto a lightly floured surface and knead for 2 minutes until smooth, then pat the dough out until its 2cm (1 inch) thick.

5. Dust a 5cm (2 inch) plain metal cutter with flour and use it to stamp out the rounds. (Push the cutter down firmly. Do not twist it or the scones may rise unevenly.)

6. Transfer the scones to a floured baking sheet. Dust the scones lightly with flour.

7. Place the baking tray in a preheated oven and bake for 15 minutes or until well risen and golden.

8. Transfer to a wire rack and leave to cool.

➤ *Serve with clotted cream, jam and a cup of tea.*

Eccles Cakes

Filling

80g (3 oz)	unsalted butter
1	orange
140g (5 oz)	soft brown sugar
140g (5 oz)	currants
1 tsp	ground cinnamon
½ tsp	ground nutmeg
1 tbs	orange zest
60g (2 oz)	mixed citrus peel

1. Melt butter in a saucepan over a low heat. Once melted, remove from heat.

2. Juice the orange and stir into butter. Add the remaining ingredients and mix well. Set aside to cool.

Pastry

1 block of 400g (14 oz)	ready-made puff pastry
	milk for glazing
	caster sugar for dusting

Preheat oven to 220°C/425°F/Gas 7

1. Roll out pastry on a lightly floured work surface to a thickness of approximately 3mm (⅛ inch). Using a 6cm (2½ inch) cutter cut the pastry into rounds.

2. Place 1 tsp of the filling in the middle of each round, then brush the edges of half the pastry with milk. Bring the other half of the pastry over and seal.

3. Bring the corners of the pastry up into the middle and pinch to seal.

4. Turn the sealed pastry parcel over so that the seam is underneath. Gently roll out until it is about ½cm (¼ inch) thick. Gently pat back into a round shape and place onto a greased baking tray.

5. Make 3 small slits on top of each cake and brush with milk and sprinkle with caster sugar.

6. Place the baking tray in a preheated oven and bake for 15 minutes or until the pastry is golden-brown and puffed up.

7. Transfer the cakes to a wire rack to cool.

➡ *Dust with icing sugar before serving.*

Chocolate Truffles

300g (11 oz)	dark plain chocolate
3 tbs	butter
180ml (6 fl oz)	cream
100g (4 oz)	blanched almonds
100g (4 oz)	desiccated coconut
	cocoa powder for coating

Method

1. Add chopped chocolate, butter and cream into a saucepan. Cook gently over a low-medium heat, allowing the chocolate to melt, but taking care not to boil.

2. Place the mixture in the fridge to cool for one hour. The chocolate should become evenly cooled and firm, but not set.

3. Add finely chopped almonds and coconut into the chocolate mixture. Combine until evenly distributed then create the truffles by shaping the mixture into small balls.

4. Put a little cocoa powder in a small bowl and dip the truffles in, rotating each one until evenly coated. The truffles can be stored in the fridge in an airtight container for 2–3 days or frozen until needed.

Chili Chocolate Truffles

1 tbs	red chilli

At step 1, add 1 tbs of finely chopped, deseeded red chilli to the pan while melting chocolate.

Blueberry Fool

300g (11 oz)	blueberries
50g (2 oz)	caster sugar
1 tbs	water
140ml (5½ fl oz)	double cream
200ml (7 fl oz)	crème fraîche
1 tsp	icing sugar

Method

1. Set aside a few blueberries for decoration. Add the remaining blueberries, caster sugar and water into a saucepan and heat on low-medium for 8–10 minutes or until the sugar dissolves, the berries release their juice and are soft.

2. Crush blueberries with a fork to form compote then set aside to cool.

3. Pour double cream and crème fraîche in a bowl and whisk for 2–3 minutes, until the mixture becomes fairly firm.

4. Stir in icing sugar and ¾ of the blueberry compote, then lightly fold in the remaining crushed blueberries to create a ripple effect.

5. Divide the mixture between 4 glasses and chill.

➤ *Serve with a layer of berries.*

Bread & Butter Pudding

Serves 6

30g (1 oz)	butter
8 slices	thin sliced bread
50g (2 oz)	sultanas
2 tsp	ground cinnamon
300ml (10½ fl oz)	whole milk
150ml (5½ fl oz)	double cream
1	vanilla pod
2 tsp	cornflour
30g (1 oz)	granulated sugar
¼ tsp	ground nutmeg

Preheat oven to 180°C/350°F/Gas 4

Method

1. Grease a 1 litre (34 fl oz) baking dish with butter.

2. Remove the crust from the bread slices, then spread butter thinly on one side of each slice and cut each slice into four triangles.

3. Layer the bread, butter-side up, in the bottom of the dish. Add a light layer of sultanas and sprinkle with cinnamon. Repeat layers, finishing with a layer of bread.

4. Pour milk and cream into a saucepan and gently warm over a low heat. Split vanilla pod in half and scrape out the seeds. Add the seeds and the open pod to the pan and continue to heat until the milk is about to boil.

5. Mix cornflour with a drop of milk in a measuring jug, stirring to create a smooth paste. Pour some heated milk and cream to the paste in measuring jug, stir well, and pour back into the pan. Add 18g of sugar and lightly whisk with fork over the heat until custard slightly thickens.

6. Remove from heat and pour the custard over the bread layers. Sprinkle with nutmeg and the remaining sugar, then leave to stand for 30 minutes.

7. Place the baking dish in a preheated oven and bake for 30–40 minutes or until the custard has set and the top is golden brown.

Christmas Bread & Butter Pudding

1	orange
1	lemon
30g (1 oz)	cranberries

At step 3, add cranberries with the sultanas.
At step 5, add the zest of an orange and lemon into the custard.

Honeycomb

1 tbs	vegetable oil
80g (3 oz)	butter
160g (6 oz)	caster sugar
80g (3 oz)	golden syrup
2 tsp	bicarbonate of soda

Method

1. Grease a 20cm (8 inch) square baking tin with vegetable oil.

2. Add the butter, sugar and golden syrup into a saucepan and warm on a low heat until the sugar has dissolved.

3. Turn up the heat and boil rapidly, without stirring. If the mixture goes darker in one area, gently swirl the saucepan to mix together. Keep boiling for 5 minutes or until the mixture becomes golden brown.

4. Add bicarbonate of soda to the mixture and stir for a few seconds. Take care, the mixture will fizz and expand.

5. Pour the honeycomb mixture into the baking tin and set aside until cooled and set.

➤ *Break into small pieces and sprinkle over desserts.*

Blueberry & Polenta Fairy Cakes

Makes 14

110g (4oz)	unsalted butter
110g (4oz)	demerara sugar
125g (4½oz)	soft light brown sugar
2 tbs	apple cider vinegar
160g (6oz)	plain flour
140g (5oz)	fine ground polenta
½ tsp	bicarbonate of soda
½ tsp	baking powder
¼ tsp	salt
125ml (4½ fl oz)	buttermilk
125g (5oz)	fresh or frozen blueberries

Preheat oven to 180°C/350°F/Gas 4

Method

1. Add butter and sugar into a bowl and cream using a whisk for approximately 3–5 minutes.

2. Pour in the apple cider vinegar, adding a little at a time, mixing well after each addition.

3. Add sifted plain flour, polenta, bicarbonate of soda, baking powder and salt into a bowl. Add one-third of the flour mixture to the creamed mixture and beat until combined.

4. Add half the buttermilk and beat until combined. Add another one-third of the flour mixture and beat. Add remaining buttermilk and beat. Add the last one-third of the flour mixture and beat until combined.

5. Toss the blueberries gently in a little plain flour before folding them into the batter. This prevents the blueberries from shrinking in the fairy cakes.

6. Spoon the mixture into 14 cupcake cases, filling two-thirds of the case. Set the cupcake cases in a muffin tray.

7. Place the muffin tray in a preheated oven and bake for 25 minutes or until slightly raised and golden brown. Insert a skewer into a cake, if cooked the skewer will come out clean.

8. Remove the muffin tray from the oven and cool for 10 minutes then transfer the cupcakes from the tray to a wire rack.

➤ *Serve warm with butter, fresh blueberries and a dusting of icing sugar.*

Lemon Fairy Cakes

Fairy Cakes

110g (4 oz)	unsalted butter
225g (8 oz)	golden caster sugar
2 tbs	apple cider vinegar
150g (5 oz)	self-raising flour
150g (5 oz)	plain flour
90 ml (3½ fl oz)	semi-skimmed milk
2 tbs	lemon juice
1 tbs	sour cream
1 tsp	lemon zest

Preheat oven to 180°C/350°F/Gas 4

1. Add butter and sugar in a bowl; cream for 3-5 minutes using a blender or until smooth.

2. Add apple cider vinegar a little at a time, beating well using a fork.

3. Sift and combine both self-raising and plain flours in a separate bowl.

4. Pour milk into a jug and add lemon juice and sour cream and set aside

5. Add one-third of the flour into the creamed mixture and beat well, then pour in one-third of the milk mixture and beat again. Repeat these steps until all the flour and milk mixture has been added, adding lemon zest with the last one-third of flour. If the mixture starts to curdle, add another spoonful of plain flour and beat well.

6. Spoon the mixture into 12 cupcake cases, filling two-thirds of the case. Set the cupcake cases in a muffin tray.

7. Place the muffin tray in a preheated oven and bake for 25 minutes or until slightly raised and golden brown. Insert a skewer into a cake, if cooked the skewer will come out clean.

8. Remove the muffin tray from the oven and cool for 10 minutes then transfer the cupcakes from the tray to a wire rack.

Lemon Buttercream Icing

110g (4oz)	unsalted butter
2 tbs	lemon juice
2 tsp	lemon zest
500g (1 lb 2oz)	icing sugar

1. Add butter, lemon juice, grated lemon zest and half of the icing sugar into a mixing bowl. Mix the ingredients using a blender until smooth. Gradually add the remainder of the icing sugar and beat again until the buttercream is smooth and creamy.

2. Decorate the cakes with the lemon buttercream.

➤ *Serve topped with sugared lemon slices or grated lemon zest.*

Vanilla Fairy Cakes

Fairy Cakes

110g (4oz)	unsalted butter
300g (11oz)	self-raising flour
125ml (4½ floz)	buttermilk
1 tsp	vanilla extract
1 tsp	bicarbonate of soda
½ tsp	salt
220g (8oz)	caster sugar
125ml (4½ floz)	hot water
1 tbs	apple cider vinegar

Preheat oven to 180°C/350°F/Gas 4

1. Line a 14 cupcake cases in a muffin tray. Add 2 tbs of water to each of the empty remaining muffin wells.

2. Add the ingredients in a bowl, leaving apple cider vinegar last. Beat the mixture using a food processor or blender until smooth.

3. Spoon the batter into the cupcake cases. Place the muffin tray into a preheated oven and bake for 20–25 minutes or until risen and golden brown. Insert a skewer into a cake, if cooked the skewer will come out clean.

4. Remove the muffin tray from the oven and cool for 10 minutes then transfer the cupcakes from the tray to a wire rack. Allow the cakes to cool down completely.

Icing

375g (13 floz)	icing sugar
3 tbs	cocoa powder
2 tbs	milk
2 tbs	buttermilk
4 tbs	unsalted butter
1 tsp	vanilla extract
¼ tsp	salt

1. Add the ingredients in a bowl and combine using a blender until creamy and smooth.

2. Spread the icing over each fairy cake using a spoon.

Vegan Chocolate Fairy Cakes

Makes 12

Fairy Cakes

300g (11 oz)	plain flour
150g (5 oz)	granulated sugar
70g (3 oz)	unsweetened cocoa
¾ tsp	bicarbonate of soda
½ tsp	salt
250ml (9 fl oz)	water
80ml (3½ fl oz)	sunflower oil
1 tbs	apple cider vinegar
1½ tsp	vanilla extract

Preheat oven to 180°C/350°F/Gas 4

1. Add sifted flour, cocoa, sugar, bicarbonate of soda and salt in a bowl and mix well. Add water, oil, vinegar and vanilla into the bowl and whisk until the batter is smooth.

2. Spoon the mixture into 12 cupcake cases, filling two-thirds of the case. Set the cupcake cases in a muffin tray.

3. Place the muffin tray in a preheated oven and bake for 20–25 minutes or until golden and slightly risen. Insert a skewer into a cake; if cooked, the skewer will come out clean.

4. Remove the muffin tray from the oven and cool for 10 minutes then transfer the cupcakes from the tray to a wire rack.

Frosting

190g (7 oz)	icing sugar
3 tbs	dairy free margarine
1–2 tbs	unsweetened soya milk
½ tsp	vanilla extract
85g (3 oz)	dairy free chocolate

1. Add icing sugar, margarine, 1 tbs soya milk and vanilla in a bowl and beat until smooth. Add chocolate and beat until the frosting is light, fluffy and spreadable, adding remaining soya milk as required. Spread frosting on fairy cakes.

Strawberry Fairy Cakes

Makes 8

Fairy Cakes

I	lemon
125g (5 oz)	unsalted butter
125g (5 oz)	caster sugar
½ tsp	vanilla extract
65g (2 oz)	plain or spelt flour
65g (2 oz)	ground almonds
¾ tsp	baking powder
3 tbs	milk

Preheat oven to 200°C/400°F/Gas 6

1. Grate the zest of one lemon. Add the zest, butter, sugar, vanilla extract, flour, almonds and baking powder into a food processor and mix until smooth.

2. Add milk, I tbs at a time, until the mixture is of a soft dropping consistency.

3. Spoon the mixture into 8 cupcake cases, filling two-thirds of the case. Set the cupcake cases in a muffin tray.

4. Place the muffin tray in a preheated oven and bake for 15–20 minutes or until golden and slightly risen. Insert a skewer into a cake; if the cake is cooked, the skewer will come out clean.

5. Remove the muffin tray from the oven and cool for 10 minutes then transfer the cupcakes from the tray to a wire rack.

6. Pierce a whole in the top of each cake and scoop out a little of the cake to create a hollow in the centre and set aside.

Topping

150g (5 oz)	mascarpone cheese
4 tbs	crème fraîche
3 tbs	icing sugar
I tbs	lemon juice
225g (8 oz)	strawberries

1. Put the mascarpone, crème fraîche, icing sugar and freshly squeezed lemon juice in a bowl and beat with a wooden spoon until smooth and set aside.

2. Set aside 8 small strawberries for decoration. Chop the remaining strawberries into small pieces. Stir the chopped strawberries into the cream to form a marbled pink effect, do not over mix the ingredients.

3. Fill the hollows of the fairy cakes with the strawberry cream.

➤ *Serve topped with a strawberry and dusting of icing sugar.*

Gingerbread Men

Biscuit

80ml (3½ fl oz)	sunflower oil
165g (6 oz)	golden caster sugar
60ml (2 fl oz)	soya milk
400g (14 oz)	plain flour
½ tsp	baking soda
½ tsp	baking powder
½ tsp	salt
½ tsp	ground nutmeg
½ tsp	ground cloves
½ tsp	ground cinnamon
1½ tsp	ground ginger

Preheat oven to 180°C/350°F/Gas 4

1. Lightly grease baking tray or line a baking tray with parchment paper.

2. Put oil and sugar in a bowl and blend for approximately 3 minutes. Add soya milk and blend, the molasses and soya milk will not really blend with the oil.

3. Add sifted flour, baking soda, baking powder, salt, nutmeg, cloves, cinnamon and ginger into the bowl, mixing into a stiff dough.

4. Flatten the dough into a disk, wrap in cling-film and chill in the fridge for an hour or up to 3 days. If chilled for longer than an hour, let the dough sit for 10 minutes to warm up before proceeding.

5. Turn out the dough onto a lightly floured surface and roll the dough to a thickness of 5mm (¼ inch). Cut out shapes with cookie cutters and gently place on the baking sheets using a spatula.

6. Place the baking tray in a preheated oven and bake for 8 minutes. Remove from oven and cool for 2 minutes on the baking sheet and then move to a cooling rack.

Icing

190g (7 oz)	icing sugar
4 tbs	soya milk

1. Add icing sugar and milk in a bowl and beat until a smooth and spreadable cream is formed. Once cookies have cooled, spread icing on the cookies.

Jam Tart

Makes 12

100g (4 oz)	butter
250g (9 oz)	plain flour
¼ tsp	salt
2–3 tbs	cold water
370g (13 oz)	strawberry jam, fruit jam or lemon curd

Preheat oven to 180°C/350°F/Gas 4

Method

1. Lightly grease a 12 hole tart mould with butter.

2. Cut the butter into small cubes and place in a bowl adding flour and salt. Using your fingertips, rub butter into the flour until the mixture resembles fine breadcrumbs, mixing as quickly as possible to prevent the dough becoming warm.

3. Add water to the mixture and, using a cold knife, stir until the dough binds together. Add more cold water, 1 tsp at a time, if the mixture is too dry.

4. Wrap the dough in cling film and chill in the fridge for a minimum of 15 minutes and a maximum of 30 minutes.

5. Alternatively, the dough can also be made in a food processor by mixing the flour, butter and salt in the bowl of the processor on a pulse setting. Once the mixture resembles breadcrumbs, add water slowly through the funnel until the dough comes together in a ball. Wrap in cling film and chill as above.

6. Unwrap the pastry and turn out onto a lightly floured work surface and roll the pastry to ½cm (¼ inch) thickness. Using a tart cutter or cup, cut circles in the pastry just slightly bigger than the holes in the prepared tart mould. Gently press 1 disc into the tart mould.

7. Place a heaped teaspoon of jam or lemon curd into the pastry lined tart mould. Be careful not to overfill, as the jam will spill out when hot and burn.

8. Repeat until all the pastry is used up. Pastry trimmings can be combined with the rest of the pastry and rerolled several times.

9. Place the tart mould in a preheated oven and bake for 15 minutes or until golden brown. Remove from the oven and leave to cool completely.

Desserts

179

Glazed Rhubarb Tart

400g (14oz)	ready-made puff pastry
6–8 stalks	rhubarb
5 tbs	apple or redcurrant jelly
1 tbs	water
	soya milk to bind

Preheat oven to 200°C/400°F/Gas 6

Method

1. Turn the pastry out onto a lightly floured surface. Roll out the pastry to approximately 25cm x 30cm (10 x 12 inches). Prick the pastry all over with a fork, this will stop the pastry from over puffing when placed in the oven. Drape the pastry over a rolling pin and unroll it onto a lined baking tray.

2. Wash and cut rhubarb into 5cm (2 inch) sticks then arrange into rows in the centre of the pastry.

3. Brush the edges of the pastry with milk or soya milk, then pick up and pinch the corners together to enclose the tart.

4. Place the baking tray in a preheated oven and bake for 20–30 minutes or until the pastry is golden and the rhubarb soft. Remove from the oven and place onto a cooling rack.

5. Melt the jelly in a saucepan over low-medium heat, adding 1 tbs of water. Bring to boil so the jelly becomes runny. Brush several layers of jelly over the tart until glossy.

➤ *Serve at room temperature with ice cream or soya cream.*

Summer Pudding

500g (1 lb 2oz)	mixed blackberries and blackcurrants
3 tbs	clear honey or maple syrup
110g (4oz)	raspberries
110g (4oz)	strawberries
8 slices	white bread

Method

1. Place blackberries, blackcurrants and honey in a saucepan on a low-medium heat and cook for 10–15 minutes or until tender, stirring occasionally. Add raspberries and strawberries and leave to cool. Strain the fruit, reserving the juice in a bowl.

2. Remove crust from the bread slices. Take 3 slices of bread and cut 3 circles to fit the base, middle and top of a 900ml (31½ fl oz) pudding basin. Cut the remaining bread slices into triangular wedges.

3. Soak all the bread in the reserved fruit juice.

4. Line the bottom of the pudding basin with the smallest circle of bread then arrange the triangle shaped bread around the side. The tips of the bread triangles will be sticking up from the top of the bowl at this stage.

5. Pour in half the fruit and place the middle-sized circle of bread on top. Cover with the remaining fruit then top with the largest bread circle. Fold over any bread protruding from the basin.

6. Cover the top of the fruit with more bread wedges. Place the pudding basin on a plate to collect any juices.

7. Cover the pudding basin with a saucer small enough to fit inside and put a 450g (1 lb) weight on top. Leave in the fridge overnight.

8. Turn out onto a serving plate and pour over any remaining fruit juice.

➤ *Serve with lactose free whipped cream or soya cream.*

Sticky Toffee Pudding

Serves 4

Sponge

200g (7 oz)	dates
250ml (9 fl oz)	milk
100ml (3½ fl oz)	water
1 tsp	bicarbonate of soda
115g (4 oz)	butter
115g (4 oz)	soft brown sugar
3 tbs	golden syrup
200g (7 oz)	self-raising flour
⅛ tsp	ground nutmeg
½ tsp	ground ginger
½ tsp	ground cinnamon
1 tsp	vanilla extract

Preheat oven to 190°C/375°F/Gas 5

1. Line a 20cm x 20cm (8 x 8 inch) shallow cake tin with baking parchment.

2. Chop dates in half, place in a saucepan and cover with milk and water. Place saucepan on heat and simmer for 3–4 minutes or until the dates are soft.

3. Remove from the heat and stir in bicarbonate of soda, which will froth when added. Set aside and leave to cool.

4. Add butter, sugar and golden syrup into a bowl and beat together until the mixture is creamy. Add the date mixture and stir in.

5. Add sifted flour, ground nutmeg, ginger and cinnamon to the date mixture and fold.

6. Spoon the sponge mixture into the prepared cake tin.

7. Place the cake tin in a preheated oven and bake for 30 minutes or until cooked and the sponge bounces back when pressed.

Sauce

1 tbs	golden syrup
55g (2 oz)	butter
55g (2 oz)	dark muscovado sugar
2 tbs	black treacle
110ml (4 fl oz)	double cream

1. Melt syrup, butter, sugar and treacle in a saucepan on low-medium heat and simmer for 5 minutes, stirring occasionally. Leave to cool slightly then stir in double cream.

2. Prick the pudding all over and pour half the hot toffee sauce over the pudding.

➤ Serve with the remaining sauce and a scoop of vanilla ice cream.

Victoria Sponge

75g (3 oz)	margarine
175ml (6 fl oz)	hot water
1–2 tbs	golden syrup
½ tsp	bicarbonate of soda
225g (8 oz)	self-raising flour
75g (3 oz)	caster sugar
1 tsp	vanilla extract
370g (13 oz)	strawberry or raspberry jam
300ml (10½ fl oz)	whipped cream

Preheat oven to 190°C/375°F/Gas 5

Method

1. Grease sides and base of two 18cm (7 inch) baking tins.

2. Add the margarine and hot water into a saucepan and allow the margarine to melt. Add golden syrup and bicarbonate of soda and stir well.

3. Add sifted flour and sugar in a bowl and mix well.

4. Add the liquid mixture and vanilla extract to the flour mixture beating well. The mixture should form a batter. Pour the batter evenly into the baking tins.

5. Place the baking tins in a preheated oven and bake for 15–20 minutes or until golden brown.

6. Remove the baking tins and allow the cakes to cool down on a wire rack.

7. Once cool, spread generous amounts of jam on 1 of the cakes. Add a layer of whipped cream and place the other sponge on top to sandwich.

➥ *Serve dusted with icing sugar and cream or ice cream.*

White Chocolate & Raspberry Mud Cake

Lf V

Serves 8–10

200g (7 oz)	white chocolate
200g (7 oz)	margarine
250ml (9 fl oz)	milk
170g (6 oz)	caster sugar
400g (14 oz)	self-raising flour
1 tsp	baking powder
1 tsp	bicarbonate of soda
60ml (2 fl oz)	water
2 tbs	apple cider vinegar
2 tsp	vanilla extract
2 tsp	lemon juice
200g (7 oz)	frozen raspberries

Preheat oven to 165°C/325°F/Gas 3

Method

1. Place chocolate, margarine, sugar and 190ml (7 fl oz) of milk in a saucepan over a low heat. Whisk continuously until the ingredients have melted.

2. Add sifted flour, baking powder and bicarbonate of soda in a bowl and mix well.

3. Add water, cider vinegar and vanilla extract to the chocolate mixture and mix well.

4. Add half of the chocolate mixture to the flour stirring until smooth then repeat until all are combined.

5. Combine remaining milk and lemon juice in a jug and set aside for a few minutes until it curdles. Once the milk has curdled, add to the bowl then add the raspberries and mix thoroughly.

6. Pour mixture into pre-greased floured cake tin. Place the cake tin a in a preheated oven and bake for 1 hour 20 minutes. Once cooked, allow the cake to cool gradually before turning out onto a wire rack.

Trifle

Serves 6–8

Sponge

115g (4 oz)	self-raising flour
40g (1 oz)	caster sugar
40g (1 oz)	margarine
1 tbs	golden syrup
90ml (3½ fl oz)	hot water
¼ tsp	bicarbonate soda

Preheat oven to 190°C/375°F/Gas 5

1. Sift flour in a bowl and mix in caster sugar.

2. Add margarine, syrup and hot water in a separate bowl. Once the margarine and syrup have melted add the bicarbonate of soda and mix well.

3. Pour the margarine mixture into the flour mixture and beat thoroughly.

4. Pour the mixture into a greased baking tin. Place in a preheated oven and bake for 12–15 minutes or until the sponge is firm to touch.

5. Remove from the oven, and place the tin on a cooling rack.

6. Once sponge has cooled down, remove from tin and set into the bottom of a large glass bowl.

Trifle

1 packet of 85g (3 oz)	strawberry jelly
100g (4 oz)	raspberries
100g (4 oz)	strawberries
570ml (1 pint)	custard
300ml (10½ fl oz)	whipping cream
100g (4 oz)	toasted almond slices
200g (7 oz)	glacé cherries
200g (7 oz)	chocolate

1. Make vegetarian jelly according to instructions on the packet. Add berries and let it set. Once the jelly has set, spoon onto sponge.

2. Make custard according to instructions on the packet, allow to cool and pour over the jelly.

3. Whip the cream until thick and layer over the custard. Decorate with almonds, cherries and grated chocolate.

Treacle Sponge Pudding

Pudding

2 tbs	golden syrup
2 tbs	lemon juice
2 tbs	breadcrumbs
110g (4 oz)	butter
110g (4 oz)	golden caster sugar
150g (3 oz)	self-raising flour
½ tsp	ground ginger
1	lemon
2 tbs	apple cider vinegar
2 tbs	milk

1. Grease the bottom of a 600ml (21 fl oz) pudding bowl with butter.

2. Mix syrup with lemon juice and breadcrumbs in a bowl. Spoon the mixture around the base of the pudding bowl.

3. Cream the butter in a bowl, then add caster sugar and beat until light and fluffy.

4. Stir in flour, ginger and the zest of 1 lemon.

5. Stir apple cider vinegar into milk in a separate bowl. Add enough milk to the pudding to make a soft mixture.

6. Pour the mixture into the pre-greased pudding basin with a lid of greaseproof paper tied on with string. Cover and steam for 1 hour 15 minutes.

7. After steaming, remove the bowl from the pan carefully and let it stand for 5 minutes. Remove the paper and carefully turn the bowl upside down onto a warm plate.

Sauce

3 tbs	golden syrup
3 tbs	lemon juice

1. Add golden syrup in a saucepan and warm over low heat and mix in the lemon juice. Pour sauce over the top of the pudding.

➤ *Serve with whipped cream or custard. To reheat, steam for 40 minutes to soften.*

Treacle Tart

Serves 6

Pastry

225g (8 oz)	plain, self-raising or spelt flour
110g (4 oz)	margarine
¼ tsp	salt
2 tbs	water

Preheat oven to 200°C/400°F/Gas 6

1. Set aside an ungreased ovenproof glass dish or baking tray 20–23cm (8–9 inches) wide.

2. Add sifted flour, margarine and salt into a bowl. Using your fingertips rub the margarine into the flour until the mixture resembles fine breadcrumbs. Mix in water to make firm dough.

3. Turn the dough out onto a lightly floured surface, and roll out the pastry into a circle, approximately 4cm (1½ inches), larger than the tart plate. Cut a strip 2½cm (1 inch) wide around the edge of the pastry.

4. Brush the rim of the tart plate with water. Lift the round of pastry on the rolling pin. Place on the tart plate and press down gently.

5. Trim off further surplus pastry from around the edge of the plate using a sharp knife. Press your thumb around the top outer edge of the pastry to make a wavy pattern.

Filling

3 tbs	golden syrup
3 tbs	breadcrumbs
1	lemon

1. Juice and grate the zest of 1 lemon then add to a saucepan. Add golden syrup, and breadcrumbs, into the saucepan and warm over a low heat until the syrup melts. Remove the saucepan from heat. Once the liquid mixture has cooled down, spread over the pastry, leaving the rim clear.

2. Make the remaining pastry into a ball. Roll out thinly. Cut into narrow strips long enough to crisscross over the filling.

3. Brush the ends of the strips with water and arrange in a crisscross pattern across the filling, pressing the wet ends against the outside edge of the pastry.

Desserts

The strips can be twisted for a more interesting pattern or can be cooked without the pastry pattern.

4. Place the baking tray in a preheated oven and bake the pastry for 30–35 minutes.

➧ *The tart can be eaten hot or cold, served with clotted cream.*

Jam Tart

    2–3tbs   jam

At step 1, for the filling, heat 2–3 tbs of jam gently in a saucepan to smooth out. Cool and pour over pastry.

Marmalade Tart

    2–3tbs   marmalade

At step 1, for the filling, smooth a layer of marmalade over the pastry.

Poached Pears & Hot Chocolate Sauce

Poached Pears

2	pears
2	cloves
2	cardamom
I small stick	cinnamon
100g (4 oz)	caster sugar
½	lemon

1. Peel and core pears leaving the stalks intact. Place in a saucepan and cover with water.

2. Crush the cloves, cardamom and cinnamon and add to the saucepan along with caster sugar and the juice of half a lemon. Bring to boil over a medium heat, stirring occasionally until sugar has dissolved.

3. Reduce the heat to low and simmer for 20 minutes or until pears are tender and the liquid has reduced and thickened.

Sauce

100g (4 oz)	dairy free margarine
100g (4 oz)	cocoa powder
100g (4 oz)	golden syrup
100g (4 oz)	brown sugar
150ml (5 ½ fl oz)	soya milk

1. Place the ingredients in a separate saucepan over low-medium heat until the butter and sugar have melted and dissolved. Simmer for 5 minutes to allow the sauce to thicken.

➤ *Serve pears with a thick layer of sauce and ice cream.*

Banoffee Pie

300g (11 oz)	digestive biscuits
110g (4 oz)	butter
110g (4 oz)	unsalted butter
110g (4 oz)	caster sugar
400g (14 oz)	condensed milk
2	bananas
300ml (10½ fl oz)	whipping cream
200g (7 oz)	chocolate

Method

1. Set aside a loose-bottomed cake tin measuring 20cm (8 inch).

2. Add butter in a saucepan and melt over low heat. Remove from heat and set aside.

3. Add crumbled biscuits to the saucepan and mix well.

4. Pour the biscuit mixture into the cake tin and press down lightly.

5. Cover the cake tin with kitchen foil and place in the fridge to set.

6. Add unsalted butter and sugar in a saucepan over a low heat, stirring continuously until the butter melts and sugar dissolves.

7. Pour the condensed milk into the saucepan and bring to boil on a low heat, stirring continuously. As soon as the mixture thickens and gives off an aroma of caramel, remove from heat and allow the mixture to cool down. Pour the caramel onto the biscuit base and leave to set.

8. Slice bananas and arrange on top of the caramel. Whip the cream and cover the banana layer, followed by a sprinkling of grated chocolate.

Caramel
At step 5, place the tin of condensed milk into a saucepan and cover with boiling water. Boil for 2 hours on low heat. Ensure the saucepan does not dry out as the tin could explode. Cool the tin in cold water before opening. Pour the caramel on top of the biscuit base and leave to cool and set. Skip to step 8.

Rice Pudding

Gf

40g (1 oz)	butter
75g (3 oz)	caster sugar
100g (4 oz)	pudding rice or short grain white rice
½	vanilla pod
1 litre (1 pint 15 fl oz)	full cream milk
150ml (5½ fl oz)	double cream
¼ tsp	salt
	ground nutmeg to taste

Preheat oven to 150°C/300°F/Gas 2

Method

1. Melt butter in a saucepan over low heat. Add sugar and stir until the butter has melted and the sugar has dissolved.

2. Add rice and vanilla pod; split length-ways. Stir until rice expands a little.

3. Pour in milk slowly, continuously stirring to prevent any lumps from forming.

4. Add cream and salt to the saucepan, allowing the rice to simmer for 15 minutes, stirring continuously. Remove from heat.

5. Pour the mixture into a casserole dish and grate nutmeg on top.

6. Place the casserole dish in a preheated oven and bake for 60–90 minutes or until there is a thin skin on the surface of the pudding. To prevent it from browning too quickly you can place a sheet of aluminium foil over the pudding.

7. Once cooked, remove the casserole dish from the oven and allow to cool.

Lemon Rice Pudding

1	lemon
½ tsp	ground nutmeg

At step 5, add the zest of one lemon and nutmeg on the top of the rice pudding.

Lemon Posset

600ml (1 pint 1 fl oz)	double cream
140g (5 oz)	caster sugar
2	lemons

Method

1. Pour double cream and sugar into a saucepan and cook over a low-medium heat, until the sugar dissolves and the cream slowly comes to the boil. Reduce heat to low and simmer for 3 minutes. Remove from heat and set aside.

2. Finely grate the zest, and then squeeze the juice of 2 lemons in a bowl.

3. Lightly whisk in lemon juice and zest into the saucepan.

4. Pour into 6 serving dishes or small glasses and place in the fridge to cool and set for 2–3 hours.

➤ *Serve with fresh berries. Alternatively, serve with ginger biscuits or shortbread.*

Parkin (Spiced Treacle Cake)

Serves 10

80g (3 oz)	oats
250ml (9 fl oz)	milk
400g (14 oz)	self-raising flour
2 tsp	baking powder
2 tsp	ground ginger
110g (4 oz)	sugar
¼ tsp	salt
80g (3 oz)	butter
125ml (4½ fl oz)	golden syrup or honey
125ml (4½ fl oz)	treacle or molasses

Preheat oven to 165°C/325°F/Gas 3

Method

1. Place oats in a small bowl and add milk. Allow the oats to soak for 30 minutes.

2. In a large bowl, mix flour, baking powder, ginger, sugar and salt and set aside.

3. Melt butter in a small saucepan over a medium heat. Stir in golden syrup and treacle until well combined. Add to the oats and milk, stir, then combine with the dry ingredients in the large bowl.

4. Stir the mixture until the texture is even, then empty out into a 20–22cm (8–9 inch) baking pan.

5. Bake for approximately 45 minutes or until the top is lightly browned.

6. Remove from the oven and leave to cool in the tin.

Christmas Pudding

1 tbs	marmalade
1 tsp	milk
1 tsp	bicarbonate of soda
1	unwaxed lemon
1	carrot
110g (4oz)	dried cherries
2	apples
350g (12oz)	plain flour
225g (8oz)	vegetarian suet or grated coconut
350g (12oz)	breadcrumbs
450g (1lb)	currants
225g (8oz)	large raisins
225g (8oz)	sultanas
110g (4oz)	mixed peel
110g (4oz)	slivered almonds
½ tsp	ground mixed spice
½ tsp	ground cinnamon
½ tsp	ground nutmeg
450g (1lb)	brown sugar
	butter or vegetable oil for greasing

Method

1. Grease 2 medium pudding basins with butter or oil.

2. Mix marmalade with milk and bicarbonate of soda in a small bowl. Set aside.

3. Zest and juice lemon, peel and grate carrot, chop cherries, and grate apples. Place in a large bowl. Add the remaining ingredients, mix together until well combined.

4. Make a well in the fruit mixture and add the marmalade mixture. Mix well.

5. Divide the combined mixture between the pudding basins. Cover them with a double sheet of greaseproof paper and a sheet of foil and tie securely with string.

6. Place the puddings into a steamer set over a saucepan of water, or use a large saucepan of water with a saucer in the bottom. Steam at full boil for 30 minutes, then reduce to a medium heat and steam for a further 1½ hours. It may be necessary to add boiling water to the saucepan occasionally to prevent it from running dry.

7. Once the puddings cool, remove the paper and foil and cover with fresh sheets of paper and foil as before.

Mince Pies

Filling

40g (1 oz)	candied fruit
¼ tsp	ground nutmeg
½	lemon
½	orange
½	bramley or cooking apple
55g (2 oz)	vegetarian suet or grated coconut
55g (2 oz)	raisins
40g (1 oz)	sultanas
90g (3 oz)	currants
85g (3 oz)	soft dark brown sugar
1 tsp	ground mixed spice

1. Finely chop candied fruit, grate nutmeg, zest and juice lemon and orange, core and finely chop cooking apple and shred suet. Put in a large heatproof bowl.

2. Add remaining ingredients to the bowl and mix well, making sure all the ingredients are evenly distributed.

3. Cover with a tea towel and leave overnight.

4. The next day, heat oven to 110°C/225°F/Gas 1/4

5. Remove the tea towel from the bowl, cover with foil and place in the warmed oven for 2½ hours. The suet will melt and help to preserve the fruits.

6. Mix well and set aside to cool, stirring occasionally.

Pastry

150g (5 oz)	plain flour
75g (3 oz)	ground almonds
¼ tsp	salt
110g (4 oz)	butter
1	orange
	unsalted butter or vegetable oil for greasing

Preheat oven to 180°C/350°F/Gas 4

1. Place flour, ground almonds and salt into a large bowl. Rub butter in, using fingertips, until it forms an even mixture.

2. Grate the zest of the orange into the mixture, then squeeze the juice of the orange into a bowl. Cut the juice into the mixture with a knife, adding just enough to bind the ingredients into a dough.

3. Lightly knead the dough until it is soft and smooth. Put it in a bowl and cover with cling film, then place in the fridge for 15 minutes.

4. Place the dough onto a clean, lightly floured surface and roll out half of it to approximately ½cm (1/4 inch) thickness.

5. Grease a large 10 slot pie tray.

6. Cut 10 circles from the rolled dough with an 8cm (3 inch) cutter and place them carefully into the 10 pie slots. Spoon in the mince filling generously.

7. Roll out the remaining dough and with a 6cm (2½ inch) cutter, cut a further 10 circles and place them to form the tops of the pies. Prick the tops gently with a fork.

8. Bake the pies for 30 minutes, or until golden on top. Remove the tray from the oven and allow to cool for a few minutes, then tap the trays to loosen the pies and slide onto a cooling rack.

➤ *Sprinkle with icing sugar and serve with double cream.*

Drinks

Gingerade

2	unwaxed lemons or limes
I (1½–2 inches)	ginger
4	cloves
I stick (2–3g)	cinnamon
220g (8 oz)	sugar
I litre (I pint 15 fl oz)	water

Method

1. Zest lemons/limes using a grater, then extract juice. Place zest and juice into a saucepan and set aside.

2. Peel and grate ginger. You will need 1½–2 tbs of ginger, use extra according to taste.

3. Place ginger into the saucepan and add cinnamon, cloves and sugar. Pour in water.

4. Bring ingredients to boil, stirring constantly. Once boiled allow to simmer for a further 10 minutes. Remove saucepan from heat and cool for 10 minutes.

5. Strain the liquid into a jug using a sieve and allow the gingerade to cool down to room temperature. Test the flavour adding more water, lemon or lime juice or sugar as required.

➤ *Chill and serve with ice cubes, sprigs of mint and a slice of lemon or lime.*

Hot Chocolate

600ml (1 pint 1 fl oz)   milk
142ml (5 fl oz)   double cream
100g (4 oz)   dark chocolate
                            sugar/honey to taste

Method

1. Pour milk and double cream into a saucepan. Break dark chocolate into approximately ½cm pieces and add to the saucepan. Bring the mixture gently to boil, whisking until smooth.

2. Add honey or sugar to desired sweetness.

➤ Serve with a topping of whipped cream and grated chocolate.

Chocolate Milk
At step 2, refrigerate, stirring a few times to avoid skin forming on top.

Serve cold.

Lemonade

3	unwaxed lemons
140g (5 oz)	caster sugar
1 litre (1 pint 15 fl oz)	cold water

Method

1. Wash and cut lemons into quarters. Place in a food processor.

2. Add sugar and half of the cold water to the food processor and blend until the lemon is finely chopped.

3. Sieve the mixture into a jug. Squeeze out as much juice as possible. Add remaining water.

➤ *Serve with ice and slices of lemon and lime.*

Limeade
At step 1, replace unwaxed lemons for unwaxed limes.

Pink Lemonade

1½	lemons
1	orange
510g (1 lb 2oz)	raspberries
300g (11 oz)	caster sugar
350ml (12½ fl oz)	water

Method

1. Wash and slice lemons and orange, then place into a saucepan and set aside.

2. Wash raspberries and add to the saucepan along with sugar and water.

3. Bring the mixture to a boil, stirring often. Once boiled, remove from heat and leave to cool.

4. Once cooled sieve the mixture into a jug. Press out as much juice as possible. The syrup can be stored in the fridge for up to 1 week.

➤ *To serve, pour a small amount of lemonade, top up with sparkling or still water, ice and a sprig of mint.*

Punjabi Roadside Chai

350ml (12½ fl oz)	water
100ml (3½ fl oz)	milk
1cm (½ inch)	ginger
4 pods	green cardamom
4	black peppercorns
¼ tsp	green fennel seeds
1 small stick	cinnamon
	tealeaves or teabag to taste

Method

1. Pour water and milk into a saucepan and bring to boil.

2. Peel and chop ginger and set aside.

3. Lightly crush green cardamom pods in a pestle and mortar and add to the saucepan, along with the remaining spices and ginger. Simmer gently for 15 minutes or until the liquid is reduced to a large cupful.

4. Add teabag or tea leaves and brew for 1 minute or longer according to taste.

5. Strain the chai into a cup using a sieve and add sugar to taste.

Elderflower Cordial

20 heads	elderflower
1.8kg (4 lbs)	granulated sugar or caster sugar
1.2 litres (2 pints 2 fl oz)	water
2	unwaxed lemons
75g (3 fl oz)	citric acid

Method

1. Shake the elderflower heads to remove any debris, then gently wash and set aside.

2. Put sugar into a saucepan with water and bring to boil, stirring until the sugar has completely dissolved.

3. While the sugar syrup is heating, zest lemons into strips of approximately ½cm and place in a bowl with elderflower. Slice lemons and add to the bowl.

4. Pour the boiling syrup into the bowl and stir in citric acid. Cover with a cloth and leave at room temperature for 24 hours.

5. After 24 hours strain the cordial through a sieve lined with muslin.

➡ *To serve, pour a small amount of cordial into a glass and top up with sparkling or still water.*

GLOSSARY OF TERMS

Al dente	'To the tooth' in Italian; cooked lightly so the food stays firm.
Bake	To cook using a dry heat that surrounds the food, generally in an oven.
Baste	To spoon hot fat or other hot liquid over food being roasted or poached in an oven, to keep it moist and juicy.
Batter	To coat an ingredient in a semi-liquid mixture before cooking.
Beat	To stir rapidly in order to incorporate air into the mixture.
Blanch	To plunge into boiling water for a short period before rinsing in cold water.
Blend	To mix thoroughly (often after chopping), especially in a food processor or blender.
Boil	To cook in vigorously bubbling water.
Braise	To stew in a closed container.
Bread	To coat with crumbs before cooking.
Brown	To cook in a pan until lightly browned on the outside.
Caramelise	To heat either sugar or foods containing it (such as vegetables) until the sugars turn brown.
Chiffonade	To stack and roll a leafy herb or vegetable into a tight cylinder then cut into thin ribbons.
Chill	To leave in the refrigerator until cool.
Coat	To cover the surface of one ingredient or mixture with another.
Combine	To add ingredients together and stir until mixed.
Cool	To set aside until cooled down.
Core	To remove the core from inside a fruit or vegetable.
Coarsely	To non-uniformly chop or grind to thick or large pieces.
Cream	To beat until fluffy and light.
Crimp	To pinch pastry or dough together.
Cube	To chop into large cubes (larger than when diced), usually measuring around 1-2½ cubic centimetres (½-1 cubic inches).

Cut in	To work a fat into dry ingredients by cutting repeatedly with a knife.
Degorge	To remove bitterness by lightly salting a vegetable after chopping it.
Deep fry	To submerge in hot oil.
Dehydrate	To remove moisture.
Dice	To chop into small cubes.
Drain	To remove excess liquid.
Dredge	To coat in a dry ingredient, before or after cooking.
Drizzle	To pour a liquid over a dish in a light stream.
Dry fry	To fry without fat or oil, removing any fat that accumulates.
Dust	To coat lightly with a fine, dry ingredient.
Flake	To break gently into small, flat pieces.
Flour	To coat an ingredient by dipping or covering it in flour.
Fold	To mix gently by repeatedly placing part of a mixture on top of the rest.
Garnish	To top a dish with an aesthetically enhancing ingredient.
Glaze	To cover with a glossy, smooth coating.
Grease	To rub with grease such as butter, usually to prevent sticking.
Grill	To cook by direct heat from either above or below.
Grind	To mash or blend into a fine paste or powder.
Knead	To work into a uniform mass by repeatedly folding and pressing with the hands.
Mash	To press or crush until smooth.
Marinade	To souse or soak in seasoned liquid.
Mince	To cut into very fine pieces (smaller than when diced or chopped).
Mix	To add ingredients together and stir until amalgamated.
Parboil	To boil until ingredients begin to soften but are not completely cooked (usually before a different cooking process).

Pare	To cut off the skin or outer layer of a fruit or vegetable.
Peel	To cut off the skin or outer layer of a fruit or vegetable.
Plump	To increase the volume of an ingredient by soaking.
Poach	To simmer in a small amount of liquid, until cooked through.
Pressure cook	To cook under high pressure in a pot with a tightly fixed lid.
Prick	To pierce, usually with a fork.
Proof	To allow yeast dough to rise before it is baked.
Pulse	To mix ingredients in a blender or mixer by using bursts of power in very short intervals.
Purée	To mash or blend until as smooth as possible.
Quarter	To cut or divide into four equal parts.
Reduce	To thicken a liquid mixture by simmering or boiling until evaporation reduces its volume.
Refresh	To pour a cup of cold water over vegetables after blanching.
Roast	To cook uncovered in the oven while coated in oil, which is reapplied periodically.
Sauté	To fry quickly in hot oil in an open pan, keeping the pan moving by shaking it by the handle.
Scald	To cook in water just below boiling point, often to remove skins.
Score	To cut narrow slits.
Sear	To fry briefly on a high heat to seal in juices, often before cooking in an oven.
Season	To improve or enhance flavour by adding salt, herbs or spices.
Section	To remove peel and pith from a citrus fruit and separate it into segments.
Set	To leave aside until it becomes solid.
Shallow fry	To fry in a small amount of preheated oil over a high heat.
Sift	To pass ingredients such as flour through a sieve, removing large grains and lumps.
Simmer	To cook in a pan over a medium heat, so that the contents are bubbling gently but not at a rolling boil.

Skewer	To pierce with a thin, pointed stick, either to check if food is cooked or as a means of serving.
Skim	To remove the top layer from a liquid.
Slice	To cut, often into thin, flat strips.
Slow cook	To cook in an oven on a reduced heat for a prolonged period.
Strain	To remove liquid by passing through a colander or sieve.
Steam	To cook in water vapour, often by suspending above boiling water.
Steep	To soak an ingredient in hot water until its flavour is infused.
Stew	To slowly cook in a liquid, using a closed pot over a low heat.
Stir	To turn or mix ingredients.
Stir fry	To cook over a high direct heat, stirring constantly (traditionally done in a thick wok).
Sweat	To heat an ingredient until its inherent moisture is drawn up to the surface.
Toss	To mix by lightly lifting and dropping repeatedly.
Toast	To brown, dry or crisp by applying a dry heat.
Whip	To beat rapidly in order to mix with air until light.
Whisk	To beat with a whisk until smooth and well mixed.
Wilt	To cook a leafy ingredient until it begins to droop.
Zest	To grate the skin of a citrus fruit.

INDEX